"The Heart Could Never Speak"

"The Heart Could Never Speak"

Existentialism and Faith
in a Poem of Edwin Muir

GEORGE PATTISON

CASCADE *Books* • Eugene, Oregon

"THE HEART COULD NEVER SPEAK"
Existentialism and Faith in a Poem of Edwin Muir

Cascade Books
A Division of Wipf and Stock Publishers
199 W. 8th Ave., Suite 3
Eugene, OR 97401

www.wipfandstock.com

ISBN 13: 978-1-62032-818-7

Cataloging-in-Publication data:

Pattison, George, 1950–.

"The heart could never speak" : existentialism and faith in a poem of Edwin Muir / George Pattison.

xvi + 98 p. ; 23 cm. Includes bibliographical references and indexes.

ISBN 13: 978-1-62032-818-7

1. Muir, Edwin, 1887–1959. 2. Religion and poetry. 3. Spirituality in literature. 4. Poetry—History and criticism. 5. Christianity and existentialism. I. Title.

BR115.A8 P38 2013

Manufactured in the U.S.A.

Contents

Acknowledgements

Although I had read some few poems of Muir's at school, I was really brought to his work by a suggestion from Bishop Neil Russell, whom Richard Holloway has called "a saintly ascetic" and described as "man who lived like a desert father; a man who had given away everything he possessed; a man who lived on hand-outs and wore only second-hand clothes; . . . a man who spent two hours every morning in silent prayer; a man who was so manifestly holy he scarcely seemed to be of the earth at all." My question to him had been whether my newfound Christian commitment meant withdrawal from the world to some kind of island existence, or whether—and if so how—one might take that commitment into the teeming life of the city and live it there. Especially, he directed me to the poem "The Transfiguration" (he was at that time living in a small religious community called the Community of the Transfiguration). Muir's poems—the work of a man who had been brought up in the islands and lived subsequently in Glasgow, London, and Prague—provided a way of negotiating that tension, and still do. For guiding me to them, I am therefore hugely and happily thankful to Bishop Neil.

The key ideas of my interpretation of the poem were worked out in two lectures given in the department of Religious Studies at Stanford University and I am grateful to Tom Sheehan for initiating the invitation that made this possible. I am also grateful to Sharon Krishek for looking at an early version of this short book and commenting on it.

Translations from non-English works not otherwise credited are my own, and I must take sole responsibility for any errors.

I am grateful to Faber Ltd for permission to quote from Edwin Muir's *Collected Poems*.

"THE HEART COULD NEVER SPEAK"

By Edwin Muir

The heart could never speak
But that the Word was spoken.
We hear the heart break
Here with hearts unbroken.
Time, teach us the art
That breaks and heals the heart.

Heart, you would be dumb,
But that your word was said
In time, and the echoes come
Thronging from the dead.
Time, teach us the art
That resurrects the heart.

Tongue, you can only say
Syllables, joy and pain,
Till time, having its way,
Makes the word live again.
Time, merciful lord,
Grant us to learn your word.

Introduction

What follows is offered as the fruit of a meditation on a posthumously published poem by Edwin Muir, named from its opening line "The heart could never speak." It is not an exercise in the kind of close reading that a literary scholar might attempt, although it will be guided word for word and line for line by the poem. Rather, it tries to do something that some literary scholars would probably regard with grave and perhaps justifiable suspicion, namely, to bring the poem into conversation with some of the leading philosophical and theological commentators of the modern period, especially those in what we may call the "existentialist tradition." Amongst these particular attention will be paid to Martin Heidegger and to such religious existentialists as Søren Kierkegaard, Nicholas Berdyaev, and Rudolf Bultmann.

The poem itself is extraordinarily simple, or seems so. Only nine of its words are more than one syllable in length, and even they are such straightforward words as "spoken," "unbroken," and "merciful." Its rhymes are as elementary as "art" and "heart," "said" and "dead," and "say" and "way." It speaks to us in simple sentences that a child could understand. What is there here that merits such extended attention and that calls for a dialogue with philosophy?

I have no ready arguments for justifying my procedure in literary terms, and, even if I hope that at least some of those who take an interest in modern poetry will recognize matters of shared interest in this meditation, it is not my primary aim to make a contribution to the study of modern poetry. In fact, I am not even looking to offer a reading of "Muir," since there are many themes, images, and poetic moves to be found in his work that I shall touch on only tangentially, if at all. Also, although I am assuming that there is a coherent poetic vision in Muir's work such that one poem can be used to interpret another, I am not committed to insisting on there being a strong, still less a systematic unity to his overall poetic production, nor shall I argue for it. That is another task, and probably one for other hands. Therefore, whilst I shall be referring to other poems to help draw out, emphasize, or deepen what I find in "The heart could never speak," it is just this poem and what it says that is my constant focus.

My strategy is guided by the rather simple assumption that, in some way or other, the poem attempts to say something "about" the human condition and, more particularly, the human condition as experienced and understood by "we moderns," an expression Muir used as the title for his first book, based on articles from the modernist journal *The New Age* and published under the nom de plume of Edward Moore.[1] But modernity in general would be much too broad a horizon to justify bringing just these philosophers, religious writers, and poets together and in the case of Muir and the existentialist thinkers there are a number of still more specific pointers to the appropriateness and maybe even the unavoidability of such a conversation. Muir was born in the 1880s and, like many of his German contemporaries (including Heidegger, born two years later), was powerfully affected by both the philosophy of Nietzsche and the poetry of Hölderlin. Unlike many of his British contemporaries, he subsequently spent much of his life on the European continent where, with his wife Willa, he would become one of the first translators of the novels of Franz Kafka and of Hermann Broch. Nor are these sources and contexts merely external to his poetry: Nietzsche, Hölderlin, and Kafka figure by name in several of them and the themes of their work—themes of time, eternal recurrence, nihilism, dread, and the relationship between this world and the realm of timeless divinities—recur at many points in his own poetry.

Heidegger spoke of Hölderlin as inaugurating a new age in poetry that he described as "the time of the flight of the gods and of the God who is to come. This is a time of need, since it stands in a twofold lack and emptiness:

1. In his Preface to this work, Muir says, somewhat strikingly, that, "The advanced have made up their minds about all the problems of existence but not about the problem of existence" (E. Moore [E. Muir], *We Moderns*, 13). In this way he identifies the theme of the essays that follow as "the problem of existence," in opposition to the "problems" that preoccupy those who are "modern" merely because of the general assumption that that is what "we" now are. Nevertheless, it is clear that whilst this may be indicative of a certain commonality of purpose with the "philosophy of existence" beginning to emerge at that time in Germany, Muir is not using the term here in exactly its Kierkegaardian or Heideggerian sense. Yet it remains worth noting.

in the 'no more' of the gods who have flown and the 'not yet' of the one who is to come."[2] This, we might say, is precisely the time of Muir's poetry—"time" or "age" in the sense not of a chronological period but of a distinctive experience of "time" itself and what it is to be in time, to endure time, and yet also to look beyond the time that now is.

There is, then, no difficulty in establishing the fact of Muir having shared significant cultural horizons with mid-twentieth-century philosophical and theological existentialists. But, of course (it will be objected), he was, after all, a poet, not a philosopher—and still less a phenomenological philosopher of the kind represented by Heidegger in the latter's breakthrough work *Being and Time.* Although the later Heidegger could come close to blurring some of the distinctions between philosophy and poetry, it seems fairly clear that there is a world of difference between just about anything Heidegger wrote and a simple poetical work such as "The heart could never speak . . ." Indeed, to subject such a work to a philosophical reading might seem to many (philosophers as well as literary critics) to repeat the kind of error made by Heidegger himself in his lectures on the poetry of Hölderlin, lectures that turn the poet into a kind of proto-philosopher. Even if it is conceded that a poem is "about" something, that is, that it is not simply a self-referential text with no external relations to the lived world of human life and experience, it is generally thought best not to approach it as being "about" ideas or arguments, i.e., the sorts of things that philosophies are generally assumed, in their way, to be "about."

I certainly hope that I shall not reduce the poetry of the poem to something that could be said just as well in the straightforward, minimally ambiguous language of philosophy. I am encouraged to think that this will not be the outcome by two preliminary reflections. The first is that the kind of philosophical and religious conversation into which I am seeking to draw Muir's poem was itself in rebellion against the idea that philosophy was solely about ideas and arguments at the expense of life. That was in part the intended force of the term *Existence* itself—a one-word programmatic statement that philosophy should begin and even perhaps end with the actual, existing human being. The second is that I am not seeking to explain Muir's poem *philosophically* or to translate it into philosophy but, precisely, to bring it *into conversation* with some philosophical and religious thinkers. In this conversation the poem will help illuminate some of the things going on in the works of the philosophers, whilst the philosophers will (I hope)

2. Heidegger, *Erläuterungen zu Hölderlins Dichtungen,* 47.

help us to see some of the wider contexts and possible force of the poem. To anticipate what this might involve, my hope is that "The heart could never speak" will help make especially clear both the proximity and the distance between an atheistic existentialism (such as that proposed by Heidegger in *Being and Time*) and the Christian existentialism that, I believe, we find in Muir. Yet the poem will, at the end, say just what it said at the beginning. It will not have changed into an essay in philosophy, and it will say what it says with as much force in words that are, as they are, irreplaceable.

The justification for this undertaking cannot, of course, be given in advance. The question is simply whether what will be said really relates to and helps us understand better what the poem has already said long since. What it says, I have suggested, is "about" something that is not reducible to the words of the poem. It is about the human condition and, especially, about the human condition in the situation of modernity. Even a first, naive reading will note such words or references as "the heart," "the Word," "time," "death," and "resurrection." It seems, then, to speak to us of the self in its deepest selfhood (the heart), of love, of time, of suffering, and of prayer; perhaps also of God. This is quite a lot for a poem of three six-line verses to be "about" and it is more than enough to motivate an attempt to interpret the poem as contributing to the question of religious existence in the modern world.

Yet it seems right to be cautious. The editors of Muir's *Collected Poems* noted that it is one of a group of poems left unpublished at his death that "needed deciphering" from the handwritten text. To Christian readers the capital "W" of "Word" in line 2 might easily—too easily?—suggest that the Word that is being spoken of here is "the Word" of the prologue to St John's Gospel, the Word that "was in the beginning with God," the Word that "was God." And even if the use of the capital "W" is assured, might this still be a case of a theoretically-driven reading going faster and further than the text itself requires? An opposite challenge is then posed by the closing lines of the poem, that are addressed to one who is named "merciful lord," with the "l" of "lord" appearing in lower case. Whilst it might suit a religious interpretation of the poem to capitalize this "L," so as to identify Muir's "merciful lord" with *the* Lord, i.e., *God* (who is also "the Word"), the lower case used here might suggest that we should or could think of this instead as no more than a hyperbolic naming of time itself. Grammatically, either interpretation is possible, so what, if anything, compels us to read it as referring to the one to whom the religious pray as *God*?

I leave that question unanswered, but comment only that the following meditation does not presume that translating the poem into the language of faith gives us the "correct" reading. Indeed, as already noted, it does not even attempt to "translate" the poem at all, neither into philosophy, nor into the language of faith. Yet my hope is that the poem will, in its way, throw some light on what an existential faith might be.

Finally, it might be helpful to point out in advance that since my interpretation attempts to follow the thought of the poem, i.e., what it is "about," and to do so by following the words as they unfold before us, it has not been possible to divide it up into neatly balanced chapters or sections. Different parts of the poem have different levels of force and extensive comments relating to the first occurrence of a word or phrase will not need to be repeated subsequently. The extraordinary declaratory force of the opening verse sets the stage for all that follows, and much time will accordingly be spent on exploring the themes it puts in play. Yet each verse introduces new and further elements, whilst the final two lines raise the tension between a worldly and a Christian interpretation to a point of consummate balance and power that calls for long reflection. In such ways the following text, like many of Muir's other poems, follows a rather sinuous path, with many twisting and turnings, but, to borrow a recurrent Muirean image, this is not merely to indulge the fascination of the labyrinth but to search for a path that leads from the labyrinth of the modern age into freedom and light.

Verse One

I

The heart could never speak
But that the Word was spoken

The Heart Speaking

The poem begins with the words "the heart." How else should a poem begin? Isn't the heart the subject matter par excellence of all poetry? To say "the heart" is immediately to invoke all that the heart means to human beings and, above all, it seems to speak to us of love. The word "love" does not, however, appear in the poem. Is it not, then, about love after all? That would be too hasty a conclusion. Love, I shall suggest, is truly central to everything said in the poem, that is, love in its more or less everyday human sense of two human beings who fall in love and who find the moving center and meaning of their lives in this world in their fidelity to that original experience of love. Putting it like that, of course, hints at how the theme of love—both in the poem and in Muir's poetry more generally—is also tied up with the theme of time. Love is not simply a once-for-all, earth-shaking, life-changing "experience": love is a relationship that is what and as it is as a relationship that endures and is always being transformed in and by time. In the poem "Love in Time's Despite," from the 1949 collection *The Labyrinth*, Muir writes of the lovers' relation to time that "we who love and love again can dare / To keep in his despite our summer still, / Which flowered, but shall not wither, at his will." Time, in this perspective, is the ultimate test of love.

Allowing "the heart" to call to mind a certain basic human experience and understanding of love, then, but postponing the further exploration of what this might mean in this particular context until we have gone several steps further into the body of the poem and, especially, till we have learned more of what Muir understands by time, a religious interpreter cannot but note that "the heart" is also a central word in the vocabulary of religion. Do not Augustine's *Confessions*, that most seminal of all religious works in the Western tradition outside the Bible, begin by reminding God and also its readers that God created us for Himself and that our hearts are restless until they find their rest in Him? And wasn't Augustine's prompt taken up and made central to the whole movement of medieval devotion and its post-medieval inheritors, from Bernard of Clairvaux through Fénelon and down to our own time? And wasn't this also the background for Pascal's famous reminder that "the heart has its reasons" and that if it is the living God, the God of Abraham, the God of Isaac, and the God of Jacob whom we seek, then the heart's reasons are a better guide than the arguments of the philosophers?

In all of this, however, tradition seems merely to be developing and reminding us of what is already said in the Bible, where the orientation of the heart is a recurrent issue in Israel's God-relationship. Didn't the prophets warn their listeners to rend their hearts and not their garments, promising a new covenant written in the heart, and speaking of a heart of flesh that would replace the stone hearts of the disobedient? Didn't the psalmist already declare that a broken and a contrite heart was of more value to God than the blood of sacrifices? And didn't Christ himself restate the teaching of Leviticus that the first commandment of all was to love God with all our heart, and soul, and mind, and strength—words that could, in a sense, be seen as expressing different aspects of a single, central human reality: the self in its most essential being? Yet, repeating the prophets' warnings against honoring God with the lips and not the heart, he also warned his listeners that it is from the heart and not from our traffic with external things that corruption issues forth. Was he not anguished by the hardness of heart shown even by his disciples? Via the manifold permutations of Christian tradition this double aspect of biblical teaching led to Kant's insistence on the heart or will as the seat both of the evil inclination in human beings and of the good will, the will to will the good that he regarded as the sole true ground of morality. Kierkegaard took this one step further when, with an additional nudge from the Letter of James, he urges that purity of heart is to will one thing and the only thing that can truly be willed with singleness of heart is the good.

There is, then, a significant ambivalence with regard to the heart in the biblical testimony. The heart can incline us to good—but also to evil. Similarly, Christian tradition speaks both of the corrupt or hard heart that makes us incapable of communication with God and, on the other hand, extols the heart on fire with love for God.

Both these aspects are beautifully and even paradigmatically expressed in the poetry of George Herbert. In the poem "The Altar" Herbert speaks of the heart as the material out of which he intends to build his personal altar to God. It is a "broken altar," however, "and cemented with tears." "Alone" (that is, without God's help), the heart "Is such a stone, / As nothing but / Thy [God's] power can cut."[1] Even more dramatically the poem "Love Unknown" tells the story of how the narrator one day brought his Lord "a dish of fruit . . . And in the middle placed my heart." To his alarm the Lord's servant to whom he presents the offering takes his heart and throws it into a font into which is falling a stream of blood "which issued from the side / Of a great rock." He is told that this drastic treatment is needed because "Your heart was foul." But now that his foul heart has been made "well, / And clean and fair" he goes on his way, until he is moved to offer one of his sheep as a sacrifice in the furnace of affliction, but, suddenly "the man / Who was to take it from me, slipt his hand, / And threw my heart into the scalding pan." This time it is because his heart was "hard." Nourished during his sojourn in the cauldron by a wine that was "most divine to supple hardnesses," he eventually escapes and makes his way home, only to find that his bed has been set with thorns, because his heart was "dull."[2] Yet for the heart that endures all these trials there is, finally, the message of "Easter," with its memorable, triumphant opening: "Rise heart; thy Lord is risen." It is the foul, hard, and dull heart that, broken and dissolved in tears, is to be raised with Christ in the resurrection and, once raised, is to "Sing his praise / Without delays."[3] Such Easter praise is, for Herbert, the basic pattern of subsequent Christian life. Better known than the poems we have been considering, thanks to its incorporation in popular hymnals, is "Praise," in which the gift of being able to sing God's praises is "the cream of

---

1. Quoted from George Herbert, *Works*, vol. 2, 19.

2. Ibid., 144–46.

3. Ibid., 36.

all [the poet's] heart," since, if he is not capable of raising God in Heaven, he is nevertheless capable, through repentance, of raising him "in my heart."[4]

The Christian heart, then, is not only the organ in which our most basic need of God is registered: it is also the organ by which we are united with God and the organ with which we are to offer on earth the praise that will also be the ultimate work of heaven. The Christian heart is at one and the same time a longing heart, a broken heart, and also a praising, rejoicing heart.

"The heart could never speak . . ." Against the background of what has just been said, we note here a hesitancy. Whether or not the heart will, by the poem's end, have learned to speak, its power of speaking is not assumed as something that is simply given: it is neither a datum nor a spontaneous capacity. There is a condition that limits this power, something that must exist or must happen if it is to speak; otherwise, it might be that it "could *never* speak." The heart, it seems, must undergo a development or transformation, it must move, or be moved, not just in the sense of being emotionally aroused but in something like the Aristotelian sense of motion as a change of state or way of being. Nothing yet suggests that this will be a change as dramatic as that of which Herbert wrote, but if we have already looked on ahead in the poem and noticed that it too speaks of the heart being broken and even resurrected, this is at least a possibility.

But before we come back to all that might be involved in Muir's understanding of what it would mean for the heart to be broken and resurrected, let us stay with a more elementary question: what might it mean for it *to speak*? How might the heart speak, and how, especially, might it speak a word of love? The question might seem almost superfluous. What is more natural for the heart to speak of than love? Yet we have only to remind ourselves of Shakespeare's Cordelia to see how this might be harder than it seems. Her name already identifies her as one destined to speak on behalf of the heart but it is precisely her *in*ability to speak her word of love to her father, Lear, that sets the tragic action in motion. "Love, and be silent," she tells herself—whereas the sisters, whose love is not from the heart, have no difficulty in speaking what seem like words of love. Many have found Cordelia's reticence insufficiently motivated, but, commenting on love's hidden life, Kierkegaard captures something of both aspects of her situation:

4. Ibid., 165.

"When the heart is full you should not grudgingly and loftily, short-changing the other, injure him by pressing your lips together in silence; you should let the mouth speak out of the abundance of the heart; you should not be ashamed of your feelings and still less of honestly giving to each one his due. Nevertheless, one should not love in word and with devices of speech, and neither should one regard them as sure marks of love. On the contrary, by such fruits or by their being merely leaves, one should know that love has not had time for growth . . . for precisely by words and techniques of speech as the only fruit of love one knows that a man has ripped off the leaves out of season and thereby gets no fruit . . ."[5]

Kierkegaard, author of *The Diary of the Seducer,*[6] certainly knew that not every word that speaks of love is truly a word of love.

Again, we are perhaps moving too quickly, since before the heart can speak of words of love it must learn in a yet more elementary way what it might be to speak at all. There is no problem in imagining lips as speaking—that is what they are for. But how can the heart, buried deep in the breast, *speak*?

In the religious context, as we have seen, the heart speaks by praising; that is, by singing: its speech is essentially song. Of course, the poet knows that human beings can speak otherwise than by singing—but such speech is not the heart's speech. The speaking forth of propositions, statements, assertions, and hypotheses, and all such modes of speech favored by philosophers are, in the end, products of the head and not the heart. Moreover, a God who is spoken of in such ways will be precisely a god of philosophers and not the God to whom the heart's reasons, sorrows, and longings are leading us.

That speaking from the heart is or has an essential kinship with singing is not only an insight of the religious poet, however. Returning to human relationships and to human love, it is often precisely as a *singer* of love-songs that the poet makes his or her specifically poetic contribution to the literature of love. For descriptions and analyses of complex relationships we might do better to go to psychologists and novelists, but for love-songs, for being sung to about love, for being sung into love—to whom should we turn but to the poets? But such common human love does not exhaust the poets' treatment of love and poetic song has often gone beyond

5. Kierkegaard, *Works of Love*, 29.

6. The central female character of this diary is, in fact, called Cordelia Wahl, a name suggesting that she is one destined to make the choice of the heart.

the exchanges of lovers and their lasses to broach the greater cosmic significance of love.

Although poets have sung of cosmic and metaphysical issues from the beginnings of Western literature (Hesiod and Parmenides, for example), the particular approach taken by modern poetry to such ultimate concerns has been largely shaped by a set of assumptions and aspirations inherited from the movement known as Romanticism. Romanticism too was much obsessed with love, but it also had ambitions that went beyond the infinite counterpoint of "romantic" love in the everyday sense of the term. The poetic word is not only to be heard in the song that the lover sings to the beloved. It is, in an important sense, a song for the world. Take Wordsworth's ode "To a Sky-lark," in which the lark's soaring song is taken as exemplary for the poet's own vocation:

> Up with me! Up into the clouds!
> For thy song, Lark, is strong;
> Up with me, up with me into the clouds!
> > Singing, singing,
> With clouds and sky about thee ringing,
> Lift me, guide me, till I find
> That spot which seems so to thy mind![7]
>
> > . . .
>
> Teach me half the gladness
> > That thy brain must know,
> Such harmonious madness
> > From my lips would flow
> The world should listen then—as I am listening now.[8]

The lark offers the poet an image in which to portray the pure vocalization of the heart, a lyric moment by which to counter the reality of a society in the grips of rapid social, political, and technological transformation and pointing to another possibility, a possibility scarcely nameable in the language of the present time. The Romantics already sensed that the coming industrial world would set in stone the already familiar division of head and heart and, unless it found resources for resistance, humanity

---

7. Despite many significant literary and political differences, we find a similar sentiment in Shelley's "Hail to thee, blithe Spirit! / Bird thou never wert, / That from Heaven, or near it, / Pourest thy full heart / In profuse strains of unpremeditated art."

8. Wordsworth, *Poems*, vol. 1, 152–53.

would be fated progressively to lose this lyric moment, and, in losing it, to lose also the capacity to give voice to what is most deeply in our hearts. In this context, the poetic word is essentially song and the poetic mission of keeping alive the lyric moment is to teach the world to sing, or, more modestly, to remind the world of song and to do so in order to keep alive the heart. Elsewhere, Wordsworth speaks even more specifically of his "last and favourite aspiration" as the production of "some Philosophic Song / Of truth . . . With meditations passionate from deep / Recesses in man's heart, immortal verse / Thoughtfully fitted to the Orphean lyre . . ."[9] The poet has something to say and to say to the world, a word of truth and therefore a philosophical word. But even this word, this "philosophical" word, is, qua poetry, to be spoken in and as *song*.[10] Heidegger, commenting not on Wordsworth but on Hölderlin and, in particular, on the poem "Homecoming: To his Relatives" also speaks of the poetic vocation as song. It is song expressive of the joy experienced by the poet as he returns to his place of origin and, in so doing, experiencing also that which is joy itself, the Holy. Yet even as he draws near to the very source of life and joy, the poet also becomes aware of what is still more mysterious, namely, the one who gives joy and whose radiance is manifest in what is holy. This "one" is beyond all naming—and therefore cannot be spoken of but only sung until the time comes when his new name can be made known to mortals condemned, for now, to this time of dearth and desolation.[11]

Muir is a poet and he is a poet whose work bears many traces both of the English Romantic inheritance and, through Hölderlin, of German Romanticism also. Is this, then, how he understands his own poetic task:

---

9. Ibid., vol. 3, 6.

10. For a full discussion of this remarkable ambition see Simon Jarvis, *Wordsworth's Philosophic Song*. Hegel too bears witness to the connection between birdsong and philosophy when he writes of birdsong that "The *voice* also belongs to the artistic drive, [the ability] to give shape to itself in the air [as] ideal subjectivity, to perceive itself in the external world. It is the birds that have especially developed this to a joyous self-enjoyment. Their voices are no mere manifestation of compulsion, no mere scream, but their song is an externalization not driven by desire, and it is ultimately determined as the immediate enjoyment of itself." A few pages later he adds that whilst horses neigh and cattle low, the bird *sings*, and, in this song, knows and enjoys its own being. The phenomenon of birdsong is thus the highest anticipation of the self-world relational structure of self-externalization and self-enjoyment that, at a higher level, is sublated and consummated in reason and freedom. See G. W. F. Hegel, *Enzyklopädie der Philosophischen Wissenschaften*, 497, 514.

11. Heidegger, *Erläuterungen*, 24–28.

to give voice to the heart by making it *sing*? And, if so, does he, like Heidegger's Hölderlin, believe himself called especially to sing what is Holy? Song is certainly not alien to Muir's poetic palette and it would be surprising if it were, not least because of his acknowledged affinities to the Scottish ballad tradition. For example, the first of two poems he wrote under the title "The Annunciation" begins with the lines "Now in this iron reign / I sing the liberty . . ." There are clearly times, then, when Muir too sees it as his task specifically *to sing*. But that is not what he writes here. Here, he considers the possibility that the heart might *speak*: "The heart could never speak / But that the Word was spoken." The heart that this poem deals with is not a heart longing to sing but to speak and to do so as a response to a "Word" being spoken. There is certainly more to be said about the tension between the poetic vocation of song and the affirmation we find here of a word that is to be spoken—that is, *said* not sung—and we shall return later to the question as to just why Muir understands the heart as needing to speak rather than sing.[12] Now, however, I want to move straightaway to the first of the poem's major interpretative cruxes.

As was mentioned in the Introduction, the printed version capitalizes the "W" of Word. To Christian readers this is likely to suggest a reference to "The Word" of the Prologue of St John's Gospel, the Word that the evangelist spoke of as being "in the beginning with God," the Word that "was God" and that, as God, was the Word "by whom all things were made," as well as being the Word that "took flesh and came among us . . . full of grace and truth" (i.e., the Word that became incarnate in the human life of Jesus of Nazareth). Is Muir then saying—as we could imagine Herbert saying—that the possibility of the heart becoming capable of speaking its true word of love is a possibility dependent on the prior act of God "speaking" to humankind in the act of Incarnation, illuminating the truth of human hearts and bringing them (back) to fullness of life?

Such an interpretation seems not to be alien to Muir. Many of his poems specifically put into play the great themes of Christian doctrine: creation, fall, and redemption. As in the second poem on "The Annunciation" or in "The Incarnate One" it is specifically "the Word made flesh" that is the locus and ultimate means of human salvation. For now, however, I shall hold that interpretation in reserve, since there is also something to be gained by looking in the first instance at the simpler reading that would see "the Word" (even if capitalized) as referring simply to the word of *human*

12. Specifically in connection with the closing lines of the poem.

speech—a word, any word, such as you or I might say to each other. But isn't this to reduce these first two lines to an empty tautology? Of course, we exclaim, the heart could never speak without a word being spoken, since nothing at all can speak without speaking a word and if, in this case, it is the heart that becomes capable of speaking, what it will speak forth will naturally be a "word." But even if this is all the poet is giving us—an empty, teasing tautology—it can still perhaps tease us into thinking (and thinking fruitfully) about just what is involved in speaking a word or, to put it otherwise, in our being the speakers of language that we are.

What It Is to Speak

It is easy to take speaking for granted. We do so much of it and some of us do it all or nearly all the time. It is the most commonplace thing in the world. But our very familiarity with language may dull us to just how extraordinary a "thing" it is. Here, then, is the testimony of someone to whom language did not come naturally. It is from the autobiography of Helen Keller who, when she was born, on 20 June 1880, was deaf and blind. Later she would become the first deaf-blind person to gain a degree and an activist in many good causes, but the precondition of everything she subsequently did was the ability to communicate with others, in language. She acquired this ability when she was seven years old, shortly after she had been put in the charge of a new teacher, Anne Mansfield Sullivan. Sullivan attempts to teach her the idea of language by getting her to touch objects such as doll, mug, and water whilst she (Sullivan) spells out the letters on Helen's hand. At first, this seems to Helen like a pleasant new game, although (she confesses) she doesn't really understand what it is about. One day, however, she smashes her china doll on the floor in a pique of rage. This is how Helen would later tell the story:

> One day, while I was playing with my new [china] doll, Miss Sullivan put my big rag doll into my lap also, spelled "d-o-l-l" applied to both. Earlier in the day we had had a tussle over the words "m-u-g" and "w-a-t-e-r." Miss Sullivan had tried to impress it upon me that "m-u-g" is *mug* and that "w-a-t-e-r" is *water*, but I persisted in confounding the two. In despair she had dropped the subject for the time, only to renew it at the first opportunity. I became impatient at her repeated attempts and, seizing the new doll, I dashed it upon the floor. I was keenly delighted when I felt the fragments of the broken doll at my feet. Neither sorrow nor regret

followed my passionate outburst. I had not loved the doll. In the still, dark world in which I lived there was no strong sentiment or tenderness. I felt my teacher sweep the fragments to one side of the hearth, and I had a sense of satisfaction that the cause of my discomfort was removed. She brought me my hat, and I knew I was going out into the sunshine. This thought, if a wordless sensation may be called a thought, made me hop and skip with pleasure. We walked down the path to the well-house, attracted by the fragrance of the honeysuckle with which it was covered. Someone was drawing water and my teacher placed my hand under the spout. As a cool stream gushed over one hand she spelled into the other the word *water*, first slowly, then rapidly. I stood still, my whole attention fixed upon the motions of her fingers. Suddenly I felt a misty consciousness as of something forgotten—a thrill of returning thought, and somehow the mystery of language was revealed to me. I knew then that "w-a-t-e-r" meant the wonderful cool something that was flowing over my hand. The living word awakened my soul, gave it light, hope, joy, set it free! There were barriers still, it is true, but barriers that could in time be swept away. I left the well-house eager to learn. Everything had a name, and each name gave birth to a new thought.[13]

To name things so they can be known for what they are and as they are, as it were, given to us that we might think about them and find in them the elements of our world, our very own life—is this not also somehow rather close to what many poets see themselves as doing? Think of Gerard Manley Hopkins' "The Starlit Night," where he urges his readers to "Look at the stars! look, look up at the skies! / O look at all the fire-folk sitting in the air," going on in the second stanza to implore us to "Look, look: a May-mess, like on orchard boughs! / Look! March-bloom, like on mealed-with-yellow sallows!"[14] It is as if the poet is trying to get us to relive our original experience of the world, as if the word might, somehow, enable us to see the stars or see the tree for what they really are.

Helen Keller's testimony also provides a surprisingly apt introduction to certain essential features of Heidegger's phenomenological approach to language, as set out in *Being and Time*. At this point, then, I move from Muir's poem to the world of existential philosophy and to one of its most seminal (if also daunting) works. In doing so, I hope we shall be able to give

13. Keller, *The Story of My Life*, 25–26.

14. Hopkins, *Poems and Prose*, 27–28.

a philosophical grounding to Helen Keller's experience that also takes us a step further in thinking of how the heart might be able to speak.

I have previously indicated the difference between the language of the heart (whatever that may prove to be) and the kind of speaking that issues in the sorts of propositions and arguments that many philosophers are mostly interested in and I suggested that this latter epitomizes what we might call the language of the head. One of the assumptions made by such philosophers, an assumption reflected also in a certain popular view of scientific knowledge, is that the job of language is to point out certain objects or states of affairs and to do so in such a way that we can consider whether what has been said is true independently of our own experience of the matter. That is to say, when I say "There's a tree in my garden" I am stating a fact that is true and that is as true for you as it is for me, even though you don't and perhaps never will see the tree itself. The statement has a truth-value that is independent of its being spoken by me. Reality, on such a view, is something "out there" that is what and as it is and all we can do is merely to report on how we find it. But such assumptions are not limited to the philosophers. If, for example, you are a doctor using the standard tests to establish whether I am mentally capable of understanding the implications of a medical procedure, you are wanting me to report on what I think or believe in essentially the same kind of way as you might ask me whether there's a tree in my garden. What I have to do is to say whether these ideas are there in my mind or not or whether I can indicate the presence of whatever it is that counts as "understanding." But whatever else is to be said for or against such an approach, it is fairly clear that it is not well suited to accounting for what we might spontaneously think of as the language of the heart. If I tell you that "I love you," I'm not simply reporting a fact: I'm exclaiming, or pleading, or promising, or despairing, or all of these and more. Heidegger, I am suggesting, understood this much better than many philosophers and can therefore help us to a different understanding of language and one that will at least take us a couple of steps further towards getting a sense for what it might mean for the heart to *speak*.

On this topic, as on so many others, Heidegger orientates himself by reference to the original occurrence of a key word amongst the thinkers of ancient Greece and to the specific meaning of the Greek term, in this case *logos*. *Being and Time* first addresses the issue of *logos* in the context of explicating the phenomenological method that the philosopher has adopted. He sees the interconnection between phenomenological method and his own guiding question concerning the meaning of Being as focused in Edmund Husserl's call to philosophers to attend "To the things themselves" instead of to the properties of merely formal arguments. Since the "things themselves" are the things as they are, Heidegger can say that "phenomenology is the science of the Being of entities—ontology."[15] The Being of entities is not to be inferred, deduced, or explained otherwise than by attending to the way in which they show themselves—and the way in which entities show themselves is, simply, as phenomena. As Heidegger explains it, the very term *phainomenon* derives from a root meaning "that which is bright [i.e., luminous or shining]—in other words, that wherein something can become manifest, visible in itself" (BT, 28 / 51). Thus, "phenomenon" "signifies that which shows itself in itself, the manifest" (BT, 28 / 51)—as w-a-t-e-r came to manifest the cold, liquid reality of water to the young Helen Keller.

Noting that there are many ways in which *logos* has been understood, Heidegger states that a basic meaning (and one which he subsequently presupposes in just about everything he says about language) is that "*Logos* as 'discourse' means rather the same as *dēloun*: to make manifest what one is 'talking about' in one's discourse."[16] "The *logos* lets something be seen" (BT, 32 / 56)—which, as he indicates, once more puts in play the verb *phainesthai* from which the word "phenomenon" itself is derived. Genuine discourse is itself therefore spoken of as "apophantic," a phenomenologization in which we are enabled to see *what* is being said from the very process of talking and in such a way that what one person says is disclosed or made accessible to the other conversants.

In this way *logos* is never primarily self-referential but points us towards a certain something, towards "what" is being talked about, and it "points" by letting what is being pointed to be seen "*as* something." Thus the truth of *logos* is to be understood primarily in terms of its capacity for making manifest and taking "the entities of which one is talking . . . out of their hiddenness . . . [and] let[ting] them be seen as something unhidden"

15. Heidegger, *Being and Time*, 37 / 61. Further references will be given as BT in the main text. The first number refers to the first German edition (reproduced in the margins in the English translation), the second to the page number in the English translation itself. "Ontology" is the technical name for the study of Being, i.e., of what it is for an entity to be, over and above how it is further qualified (e.g., as an inanimate or an animal or a conscious being).

16. Heidegger notes but does not dwell on other kinds of *logos* that do not have this apophantic function, e.g., "requesting."

(BT, 33 / 56). But this also means that *logos* is not itself "the primary 'locus' of truth" (BT, 33 / 57). Truth is not, in the first instance, the truth of judgments: *logos* enables us see things, but what seeing discovers are not propositions but how entities are. "Pure *noein* is the perception of the simplest determinate ways of Being which entities as such may possess, and it perceives them just by looking at them. This *noein* is what is 'true' in the purest and most primordial sense" (BT, 33 / 57).

Thus far we might think that Heidegger is conceiving of *logos* as the means by which human beings relate to their world. This is true—but, at the same time, language is by no means a mere instrument for helping human consciousness access external reality. When language reveals the world it also, at the same time and perhaps even more fundamentally, reveals the speaker. Now it is one of the revolutionary features of *Being and Time* that instead of representing the human being as a conscious subject standing over against its world Heidegger speaks of our typically human way of being—what he calls Dasein—as being-in-the-world. Once we understand this, we realize that the kinds of philosophical problems that involve a disembodied consciousness wondering how it can account for knowledge of objects out there in the "real" world are just wrongly conceived. We never do begin to think as a disembodied consciousness since consciousness itself arises from our life in the world. I've never known myself as not involved in the world—pushing, resisting, absorbing, acting, talking, climbing, writing, etc., etc. Therefore, because Dasein does not exist as a "subject" that "has" a "world" but exists and only ever exists as being-in-the-world, the uncovering of the world that occurs in *logos* is not simply the revelation of an object or set of objects (such as w-a-t-e-r), but, along with these, a revelation of Dasein itself: *logos*, the words we speak, reveal us to ourselves together with our world. Dasein is what it is as and by virtue of its multiple relational possibilities and it can be what and as it is only to the extent that it discovers—"uncovers"—these. World-discovery and self-discovery are inseparable.

All of this, I suggest can be read in conjunction with what Helen Keller described as a marvelous, life-changing experience. Language lets us *see* the world we inhabit, even if we are deaf and blind, and it also awakens us to our own inner life of thoughts and feelings—to ourselves. The revelation of water in the word "w-a-t-e-r" reveals language as doing something more than enabling us to formulate true propositions: it reveals the very being of the world and, as for Helen Keller, it reveals Dasein to herself, "The living word awakened my soul, gave it light, hope, joy, set it free!" she writes.[17]

But if Heidegger can help us towards a philosophical grounding of Helen Keller's experience, is there perhaps also something in her account that is missing in Heidegger's view of language? For what Helen describes is not just an encounter with the world but an encounter mediated by her teacher, of whom she writes "The most important day I remember in all my life is the one on which my teacher, Anne Mansfield Sullivan, came to me . . . to reveal all things to me . . . to love me." Of course, the discovery of language is central to the meaning of that "coming": Helen herself did not know who it was who came to her until she had acquired language. But the world-disclosing discovery of language is itself said to be owed to the teacher, Anne Mansfield Sullivan, the twenty-year old woman who gave Helen Keller the word she could not give herself. It is not just that in language, in *logos*, I am opened to the world and the world to me but that in language, in *logos*, I am held open to the world and the world is held open to me by the one—always this particular one, here, now, never substitutable—who speaks with me, who gives me their word and waits for mine. Ann Mansfield Sullivan, writing on Helen Keller's hand effects the "speaking" of the word that enabled Helen's heart to speak. It is in being loved by the one who gives me the possibility of speaking my own responsive word that I have the possibility of speech at all—and, through this possibility, of loving. To put it in a word: whilst Heidegger may provide us with an account of the

---

17. In these reflections I have followed Heidegger in emphasizing the visualizing power of language. According to the phenomenological meditation of Michel Henry on John 1, however, the power of language to represent our intuitions of the world in a kind of envisioning does not go all the way towards revealing the lived experience of life itself: the word that is and that gives life, he suggests, is a word rooted in a certain kind of passivity or suffering rather than the active illumination of Being that is at work in the apophantic word (see Henry, *L'Incarnation*, 122–32). This may reflect a theological tradition—which includes Bultmann—that distinguishes between the visual tendency of Greek thought and the opposing tendency of Hebrew thought to emphasize *hearing*. However, Jean-Louis Chrétien warns against overemphasizing this disjunction, arguing that "the task is to think how one is included in the other as in its most intimate surplus . . ." (Chrétien, *The Call and the Response*, 38). Vision too, he suggests, can also be described as a kind of listening, responding to the call in which both being and language are founded. He sees this interlacing of word and vision exemplified in Exod 20:18, where, with regard to the revelation of God at Sinai, it is said that "the people all saw voices," a formulation to which, as he shows, the interpretative tradition has been attentive, even when it has refused the terms of the biblical words themselves (ibid., 39ff.).

structure of language that allows the revelation of the heart to occur, the heart itself is somehow absent from his account.[18]

With these reflections in mind, we return to the poem and we can now see that if the heart is to become capable of speaking this will not simply be a matter of its learning to speak in a purely formal or mechanical sense so as to identify the various elements of its world. Rather, its speaking will itself be a kind of revelation—of its world, of itself, and of those with whom it is from henceforth to share its world. Moreover, its learning to speak is dependent on its being spoken to. "The heart could never speak / But that the Word was spoken" is no empty tautology but a clear indication that a heart could never speak—and perhaps would never even desire to speak—if it were alone in the world, if there were no other heart speaking to it and no other heart to which it was moved to respond. In this regard, the Jewish philosopher Martin Buber was surely right to say that the basic words in which human beings learn to speak out their way of being in the world "are not single words but word pairs," which he goes on to specify as the two (very different) word pairs I-Thou and I-It.[19] Of these, it is essentially the word pair I-Thou—a word pair that Buber defines as involving the mutual presence and mutual attention of two *persons*—that offers the true revelation of both world and self. Helen Keller's testimony, however, further underlines the correctness of Buber's sense that this basic relationship must also be understood, precisely, as a *word*, just as it confirms Heidegger's view that the word gives us both ourselves and our world in their complex interdependence.

The word and the Word

Can we stop here? Can we say it is enough for the heart simply to be spoken to by another heart and thereby be drawn into the infinitely open play of language in and through which the self and its world and the self and others are mutually illuminated and revealed for being what and as they are? Whether or not this is "enough" it is already something rather wonderful, almost verging on the miraculous, as Helen Keller's testimony powerfully shows.[20]

18. See Caputo, "Sorge *and* Kardia"; chapter 3 in Caputo, *Demythologizing Heidegger*, 60–74.

19. Buber, *I and Thou*, 53.

20. One might also think of the ending of Bergman's *In a Glass Darkly*, when David,

It is, in any case, certainly enough for an extensive philosophical meditation on the phenomenon of language as Heidegger again demonstrates, since, according to *Being and Time,* the whole sphere of language arises from within and is limited by the boundaries of finite, mortal human existence. Thus, for Heidegger, the most basic truth about ourselves and our relation to the world revealed in language is the truth that our being in the world is a being-towards-death. When our innermost conscience calls on us to attend to this truth it is no surprise, even if it sounds somewhat paradoxical, when Heidegger says that conscience is a peculiar kind of "call" that "dispenses with any kind of utterance" and "does not put itself into words at all" but "discourses solely and constantly in the mode of keeping silent" (BT 274 / 312). Why? Because the wise are those who, in the midst of a distracted world, remember their mortality and measure their speech by their constant awareness of what is and what isn't congruent with each of us having to die a singular and incommunicable death. The final word is unsayable since we can never finally say the truth about ourselves and our world if all that we have, and know, and are is forever vanishing into the silence of death. Faced with our own all-encompassing transience, we are, it seems, necessarily reduced to a definitive ignorance about ourselves and to a correspondingly definitive silence. We and our world, comprising all that is revealed in language and including our most intimate human relationships, are constantly passing away. And even if Heidegger's own decision to ground meaningful discourse in the silent knowledge of our utterly individual mortality seems to occlude the grounding of the word in human relationships (such as the relationship between Helen Keller and Anne Mansfield Sullivan and Buber's talk of I-and-Thou), one must nevertheless say that these relationships too will, in the end, fall prey to death. This does not preclude their being revealed as something rather wonderful, something almost miraculous—but it does suggest that, in the end, it is *silence* and not the word that will reign over all things.

The question of death will, as we shall see, become central to the development of Muir's poem also and we might say that one of the cruxes of the interpretation being offered here is precisely around how to understand the relationship between language and death. But this relationship is in turn intertwined with the further issue of our relationships with others,

---

until then always avoiding anything like emotional intimacy with his son, Minus, speaks to him about his feelings regarding the crisis brought on by the mental illness of his daughter Karin (Minus's sister). As the father leaves, Minus turns to camera and says, "Papa spoke to me!"

especially, as in the case of Helen Keller, with the role of others in help-ing us awaken to the world disclosed in "the word." It is with this issue we are now grappling and without in any way belittling the potential wonder of language as revealing the fragile and transient realities of our life we now turn to the interpretation of Muir's understanding of language that is suggested by the association of "the Word" with St John's Gospel. At this point we cannot say that this interpretation is demanded by Muir's poem, even if it is congruent with what we know from other poems about his use of the Christian narrative of creation, fall, and redemption. And perhaps there will be no point at which such an interpretation will be demanded or deemed to be "necessary." Yet it is without doubt a *possible* interpretation or, should we say, a possible *context* for interpretation and one that, as we proceed, will also help bring into focus further themes of the poem that we shall encounter.

Of course, many readers will resist such a move, since it seems to reg-ister a massive lack of faith in human beings and human possibilities. Who is to say we cannot speak the word that is needed to each other? Who is to say that we really do need a Word spoken to us from outside and beyond the human condition? As has just been noted, the word spoken to us by another human being can already be a kind of miracle. Towards the end of his life, pondering on the fate of human beings in an age of technology, Hei-degger famously quoted the poet Friedrich Hölderlin's words "Only a god can save us"—but isn't that kind of despair over human possibilities more indicative of the speaker's own lack of hope than of anything "objective" he has discovered about the human condition? Isn't it, in short, a typical expression of the disappointment of the old? And even if an unflinching recognition that all will end in silence may lead to disappointment and even despair, *does it have to*? Might not the constant sense of our finitude and mortality lead us all the more to value and speak well of the love we might have for one another?

We shall return to such questions in meditating on the final verse of the poem and for now I wish merely to draw attention to the possibility that it might not be a case of a sharp either / or. Much depends on how we figure the speaking of the divine Word. For Muir, as evidenced by such poems as "The Incarnate One," the divine Word is conceivable and believable only as the Word *made flesh* and incarnated in a human life. This is the Word that is the subject of the Prologue to St John's Gospel, opening "In the beginning was the Word and the Word was with God and the Word was God, the same was in the beginning with God . . . and the Word *became flesh* and dwelt among us, full of grace and truth." Yet, as Word incarnate, it cannot be alien to the intimate flesh and fabric of human life in the world. But what might it—what could it—mean to speak of such a divine Word appearing in or being spoken in human flesh?

In his *Commentary on St John*, Rudolf Bultmann, a friend and academic collaborator of Heidegger, argues that John's opening meditation on the Word should not be interpreted as if first of all there was God and then, subsequently, God made himself known by speaking his Word. Rather, John's insistence that the Word spoken in the Incarnation was the Word that "was with God and [that] was God" means that there is no way of thinking about God and no point in doing so other than by reference to this act of self-communication. How God is in speaking his saving Word to us in the Incarnation is, simply, how God is. As Bultmann puts it, "The idea of God is from the start defined in terms of the idea of revelation. To speak about God means to speak about His revelation and to speak of revelation means to speak of God."[21] However, unlike some—many—theologians, Bultmann does not use the word "revelation" as referring to something supernatural but, in a sense comparable to Heidegger's idea of language as revealing or disclosing, as simply opening up and making visible the light in which (if only we knew it!) we *already* dwell. As St John also goes on to say, the life that is in the Word is precisely "the light of men," which Bultmann understands as referring to the basic or essential luminosity of the world of human experience as such. Such a light is not an apparatus with which to see but "the brightness in which I always find myself and find my way around . . . that is, luminosity not as an external phenomenon but as the illumination of Dasein, of me myself."[22] The light that revelation bestows is not alien to human beings, since "the possibility of existence being illuminated, the salvation that comes from the bestowal of a definite self-understanding was given at the very source of existence and belongs to our existence as such. Creation is simultaneously revelation in so far as the creature has the possibility of knowing its creator and thus coming to understand itself."[23] The speaking of the divine Word, then, is simply and essentially the illumination of how and who we are in our actual existence

21. Bultmann, *Das Evangelium des Johannes*, 18.

22. Ibid., 22.

23. Ibid., 25.

and not a message from another world. Still less should it be understood as a message *about* another world.

This, then, is what is presupposed in claiming that God's Word, the Word that "is God," can be revealed or spoken to human beings living in a world bounded by finitude and death and spoken in such a way that they can understand it. Insofar as it is properly named "Word" and insofar as this Word is spoken in such a way as to reveal how we are in our being-in-the-world—therefore also revealing the possibilities open to us for self-understanding and self-transformation—it must be a properly *human* word. But this revelation is not something we can arrive at simply by attending to the call of conscience, as for Heidegger. Our existence may be illuminated at its very source but the source of this illumination is not in us and the revelation of who we really are is possible only in the light of what we might call "another light." And, for Bultmann, the Lutheran theologian, this means the revelation offered us by the historical revealer, Jesus Christ. Revelation is not a matter of uncovering a universal structure or a norm but of responding to a specific word spoken to us that demands our attention, trust, and even obedience but, at the same time, a word of liberation and fulfillment—what Christian theology calls "salvation."

This, of course, immediately confronts us with what has been called the scandal of particularity. Why *this* historical revealer? Why Jesus Christ? At one level—and as we have already heard—Bultmann does not want to say that the revelation given in and by Jesus Christ is alien to my human life in the world. "Human beings know what revelation means as well as they know what light means and as well as they can talk meaningfully of the bread or water of life."[24] Yet this does not allow us to set up criteria by which to test whether a given revelation is valid: our response to such revelation can only be on the basis of personal choice and responsibility. It is not a kind of "natural knowledge" and it cannot be *proved* that Jesus Christ is the Word of God. "The event of revelation is a question and a scandal."[25] But something similar is true of any word, any human word, that demands our trust and calls us to a new commitment. Just as we cannot *know* in advance that promises of love will be kept, believers cannot *know* that Jesus is the Christ, the Word, the revealer of God but can only bear witness to the understanding of truth that has been bestowed in their believing acceptance of this Word. The question, Bultmann suggest, is not whether we

24. Ibid., 39.
25. Ibid.

know what this revelation is but whether we want it! Although the believer's knowledge of God is spoken of as kind of seeing—"we have *beheld* his glory"—this is not a matter of seeing something supernatural shining through the flesh of the incarnate Word. The revealer does not possess any "radiant, mysterious, or fascinating" properties.[26] He is, simply, the Word made flesh and therefore, in a certain sense, concealed even in the event of revelation. All we "see" is the man, Jesus. Seeing him as the one sent by the Father, the Father's Word, cannot be mediated to us by historical experience, evidence, or trans-generational transmission (a point on which Bultmann explicitly affirms the position of Kierkegaard's *Philosophical Fragments*, which stresses the "incognito" of the Incarnation). Yet, precisely for this reason it can always once more become an entirely present word to me in my historical "now." Only in "the moment" of address and response can I "know" God and truth is therefore always and only understandable as the truth of the moment, "the now," received and interpreted by conscience, which, as Bultmann adds (further undermining the "knowledge" status of faith) can always err. And, once more, "seeing" Jesus as the Incarnate Word is inseparable from seeing ourselves in the light cast by his presence. I will never get to "know" him by making him (or seeking him as) an object of knowledge but by being open to the possibility of the gift of a new self-understanding that he has to offer and, on the basis of that new self-understanding, the possibility of a new life.

But how can this past event, the coming of the Word made flesh, reveal my existence to me now? How, to put it in Kierkegaard's terms, can it become *contemporaneous*? How can it be of the moment, *this* moment, *now*? Bultmann's own answer—perhaps unsurprisingly for a Lutheran theologian—is that it is in preaching that "the past fact is ever and again made contemporary for me."[27] And, he adds, "We thus come from a history of love in so far as Christ became the real event of divine forgiveness for human beings and really can become that in the Church's proclamation and in the faith that takes this proclamation to heart. Since Christ the word of forgiveness stands above everything that has happened and that is now happening . . . He is the Word."[28] This, of course, is nothing to do with the fervor or rhetorical skill of the preacher that makes the message "come alive" but is simply due to the fact that witness is borne. In this respect, non-Lutherans

---

26. Ibid., 40.

27. Bultmann, *Theologische Enzyklopädie*, 95.

28. Ibid.

might like to expand Bultmann's position somewhat and extend his logic also to, for example, the sacraments or to the testimony of holy lives. Yet Bultmann might reasonably respond that these can only make the divine love and forgiveness contemporaneous to the extent that they have the character of "Word," by illuminating our lives in such a way as to offer a new way of understanding ourselves and our world, and, as a word spoken to us as individuals, doing so with regard to each of us singly in our present "now." This primacy of "the Word" is not based on a narrow scripturalism but on the fundamental Word-character of existence as such—a point on which Bultmann remains in essential agreement with Heidegger, despite their other differences. At the same time, whereas *Being and Time* argues that when it comes to attaining a resolute and authentic self-understanding we have somehow to turn our backs on our fellow speakers and attend only to the "silent" voice of conscience, Bultmann believes that transformation is possible only in response to a word spoken, once-for-all by or, better, *in* Jesus as the revealer of God and made contemporaneous in the word of the preacher, who repeats this divine word to me, here, now. Only a real, other human being can address me with a word capable of saving me. I cannot speak such a word to myself by myself. And, as I have suggested, this need not be limited, as Bultmann limits it, to the word spoken by a preacher (although preachers would certainly do well to reflect that this is what their words could and even should be if they are to be genuine "sermons"[29]). Why should not someone like Anne Mansfield Sullivan do what Bultmann here confines to the preacher; that is, speak the Word that enables others to break through to the truth of their existence?

Such a Christian interpretation of what it means for "the Word" to be spoken therefore begins and ends in proximity to the interpretation that simply understands "the word" as a human word, a word spoken by one human heart to another. That a divine Word has been spoken and is the only possible ground for the speaking of such human words does not justify us in trying to by-pass either the difficult labor or the miraculous revelations of ordinary human speaking and understanding. Whatever the divinity of the divine Word might mean, its having been spoken as a "Word *Incarnate*" underlines the fact that there is no place outside human language, outside the intercourse of one human being with another, where that Word is to be heard. Its truth will be manifest and validated only to the extent that it is a

---

29. The word "sermon," of course, derives from a Latin word meaning, simply, speech, discourse or, as one dictionary has it, "anything spoken."

truth "for us," in the words we speak to one another. The Christian reading says something more than the purely secular reading, but it does not give us an excuse for turning away from the truth of that secular reading. We must become capable of speaking words of love to each other if the heart is to become capable of speaking.

II

We hear the heart break
Here with hearts unbroken

We . . . Here

The next two lines, seemingly as artless as the first two, seem suddenly to turn away from the question as to what it might mean for the heart to speak. Now it is a matter of hearing "the heart break." Of course, speaking and hearing have an obvious affinity, although it is not stated that what we hear when we hear the heart break is a word. Maybe it is just a scream or a terrible inarticulate cry. In any case, our hearts are unbroken by what we hear. We filter out the scream, if it is a scream, or do not attend to what is being said, if it is in a word that the breaking heart has spoken to us. But something even more serious than our own moral indifference to others may be at stake in such non-hearing. For perhaps speaking the word is not only a matter of speaking but also of hearing, so that a word is not really a word at all unless or until it is heard and heard as the word of a real, speaking heart. If this is so, then the heartbroken person whose word has been addressed to us will not have spoken at all until we have attended to it and recognized what is being said in it. The fate of the word, its being "a word" in the fullest sense, is dependent on the one who receives it as well as the one who speaks it (which might also be true of "the Word" in a theological sense). In not hearing the word that speaks of heartbreak we therefore effectively prevent it from being a word at all and we lock the other up in their silence all the more securely.

In any case, "we," it seems, have not yet heard the breaking heart and our hearts, for their part, remain unbroken. Good for us, we might say. Surely heartbreak is something no human being willingly or gladly endures. Heartbreak diminishes the quality of our lives and can drive a person to suicide or madness. Why expose ourselves to such traumas unnecessarily? Yet Muir will go on in the following two lines to ask that we should learn "the art / That breaks and heals the heart." That our hearts are unbroken may not, then, be a sign that all is well with us.

What, then, is being said in these two lines? The answer, I suggest, hinges on who "we" are taken to be and where "here" might be.

Muir's "we" is not accidental. As was noted in the Introduction, his first published book was entitled *We Moderns*, and the consciousness of being part of a common life and sharing a common generational identity pervades his mature poetic work. His fascination with Nietzsche has already been mentioned, but as his autobiography shows this was always from the beginning qualified by what he spoke of as his "socialism" and there is a continuing echo of the socialist "we" in his later work. Many of the poems also carry unmistakable allusions to the common history of Muir's generation and time, including its many wars and revolutions, amongst them the Cold War during which the poem we are considering was written. This, as we shall see, is integral to the force of the "we . . . here" we are now reflecting on.

In this regard, Muir is positioning his poetic stance very differently from Wordsworth. For anyone who has read their way through *The Prelude*, there can be no doubting Wordsworth's deep emotional and intellectual involvement with the tumultuous political upheavals of the 1790s, the French Revolution, and the wars that followed. Nevertheless he characteristically speaks not merely as an "I," but as an essentially solitary "I": "I wandered, lonely as a cloud . . ." or, as in "To a Sky-lark," he listens to the sky-lark precisely in order to learn what he, as an individual speaking voice, must say (or, better, sing) to the world. Wordsworth is deeply concerned about the "we" but he chooses to speak as an "I," a strategy entirely congruent with the whole shape and feel of the lyric moment he seeks to perform. Muir too will speak from time to time as an "I," as in another of the posthumous poems "I have been taught." Yet it is not unfair to say that his theme is not the fate or the vocation of the individual poet but of the "we" who, even now, share a common historical moment and it is the riddle and mystery of this common destiny that his poetic words seek to bring to light—to reveal, in the specific sense explored in the last chapter.

Muir's "we" is not, however, limited to his contemporaries. For each individual within each generation is not simply an individual but the bearer of a long history and, as such, inhabited by many voices that echo back from the most ancient strata of human life on earth. This is the theme of "The Journey Back," in which the poet ("I") sets out, as he says in the opening words of the poem, "to seek his kindred," already recognizing, it seems, that "I" cannot even be "I" unless I know who I am in relation to my kindred. These are described as "Old founts dried up whose rivers run far on, /

Through you and me." "We"—you and I and all of us together—are neither the beginning nor the end of the common history that runs through us. In that history we are the inheritors—we have actually *been*—"spoiler and despoiled" both "grinding the face of the poor" and ourselves the "poorest" of those whose faces were being ground. Our single lives are impossible except as part of this great, worldwide history that is as long and as old and as unfinished as time itself. "How could we be if all were not in all?" he asks.

For some, this might be enough. Isn't the experience of finding ourselves part of a great movement of humanity already a kind of deliverance for the solipsistic individual of the modern world? For Muir, however, this is only the first step in recognizing the truth about ourselves for, as he says in the poem, "There's no prize in this race; the prize is elsewhere, / Here only to be run for. There's no harvest, / Though all around the fields are white with harvest." As he puts it in another poem, "The Wheel," "nothing can come of history but history." Yet, at the same time, "The Journey Back" also testifies that "we have watched against the evening sky, / Tranquil and bright, the golden harvester."[30]

Experiencing our participation in the great stream of humanity is not of itself "the answer" to the problem of the alienated individual of modern times. Indeed, far from being the answer it is the experience of this common life that poses the deep human, metaphysical, and religious questions in the sharpest possible way. "Nothing can come of history but history" and if there is to be anything more than this it must lie "elsewhere," a harvest never yet gathered. But what is the reason that history is unable to fulfill itself and offer more than history? Why, to put it in a directly theological term that Muir frequently invokes, is history the history of a fall? And why can history, our common human history, not redeem us from our common fall?

In the first instance it is because we ourselves are the collective perpetrators of the violence and ill that afflict us. Reflecting on the ruin brought upon "The Good Town," Muir asks

> How did it come?
> From outside, so it seemed, an endless source,
> Disorder inexhaustible, strange to us,
> Incomprehensible. Yet sometimes now,

30. The imagery here is taken from the New Testament. On life as a race see 1 Cor 9:24–27 and Phil 3:14. On the fields being white for harvest and how this connects with Jesus's own eschatological mission see John 4:35–38.

We ask ourselves, we the old citizens:
"Could it have come from us? Was our peace peace?
Our goodness goodness?"

So, too, in "The Refugees": what we now suffer we suffer "because we watched the wrong / Last too long / With non-committal faces."

In a number of poems Muir uses the myth of the fall both to underline the point that we share in a common fate but also to remind us that this is a fate we have brought upon ourselves, difficult as that is to understand.

"We," then, means all of us, all those who were Muir's contemporaries, but along with them all who share in a common human history that, as it has evolved through time, is also a history of war, violence, and terror. This is a history in which love fails (again and again) and a history that cannot answer its own ultimate questions—even though, within this history, we are both warned and sustained by glimpses of "the golden harvester," "tranquil and bright," who will bring it to a conclusion, separating but perhaps also reconciling its good and its evil. Although there will never be a final ingathering and reconciliation within time (or so "The Journey Back" suggests), the vision of the harvester signals that time itself is not comprehensible if viewed solely as a cycle of gain and loss—a point we shall consider more fully in the next section.

We have already gone some way to specifying not only who the "we" are whose hearts remain unbroken even though they hear the heartbreak of the world, but also the "here" *where* we are. Place, like time, is a recurrent theme in Muir. In the collection *Journeys and Places*, nine of the poems have the word "place" in their title: "The Unfamiliar Place," "The Place of Light and Darkness," "The Solitary Place," "The Private Place," "The Unattained Place," "The Threefold Place," "The Original Place," "The Sufficient Place," and "The Dreamt-of Place"—titles that are in themselves indicative of some of the meanings that this theme has for the poet. "The Journey Back" too speaks of the goal as being to find "a place / Where one might say, 'Here is the starting-point,'" although, by the end, it seems there is no starting-point and the only "place" where we can ever be is the place where we are, in the middle of history, with time stretching back behind us and stretching out before us. This is precisely the place where, surrounded by fields white for harvest, we must wait for a harvest that will never come, despite visions of "the golden harvester" in the evening sky. We cannot find the way back to "the original place" nor can we yet come to the "dreamt-of" "unattained" place. Our place, even if we still have "one foot in Eden" is "the other place," a place through which we journey as "on a winter way," a place of "famished field and blackened tree" and "darkened fields." It is the "good town" whose churches have been reduced to "mounds of rubble, / And shattered piers, half-windows, broken arches / And groping arms" that "were once inwoven in walls / Covered with saints and angels" and whose "people have been scattered, or have come / As strangers back to mingle with the strangers / Who occupy our rooms where none can find / The place he knew but settles where he can."

It is "The Difficult Land," where "things miscarry / Whether we care, or do not care enough"[31] and where "the earth itself looks sad and sense-less." It is a hearth through which "A crack ran . . . long ago . . ." ("The Refugees"). And sometimes it is the Kafkaesque "Labyrinth" composed of "all the roads / That run through the noisy world, deceiving streets / That meet and part and meet, and rooms that open / Into each other—and never a final room— / Paths on the earth and tunnels underground, / And bird-tracks in the air."

If we were to give it a "local habitation and a name" (Shakespeare) it is Central Europe in the age of totalitarianism, and it is Scotland in winter, when "ice lays its smooth claws on the sill" and the sun "sweeps his arctic sword across the sky," a land "kingless" and "songless," a land "that with its dead and living waits for Judgment Day" enduring in the meanwhile a "poor frozen life and shallow banishment."

This, then, is the place where "we" are, this is "here." Yet, it seems that, despite being set in the midst of so many and so great misfortunes, our hearts are unbroken and where the heart does break "we" do not hear it. But how can we not hear the heartbreak that must be all around us in such a place as this? Of course, it doesn't need any great psychological insight to see why those in situations of great stress only too easily close their eyes to the realities of their situation, as victims of trauma blot out the memory of the traumatic event itself or use a neutral language of avoidance so as to diminish the reality of what they have lived or are living through. Similarly, those committing acts of great cruelty or wrong will mostly have persuaded themselves that what they are doing is right and is done in pursuit of one or other noble cause.[32] That we do not hear the heart break, then, is because

31. Is this a critical allusion to Eliot's prayer in "Ash Wednesday" that we might be taught "to care and not to care"?

32. See van der Post, *Venture to the Interior*, especially pp. 212–13, where the author describes how the Japanese carrying out a brutal execution on a prisoner-of-war had deluded themselves into thinking they were performing an act called for by military honor.

something within us has made us incapable of doing so—and perhaps it is simply that we ourselves are or have become incapable of speech: our inability to hear the heart break is in this case simply the obverse of the fact that we ourselves are those whose hearts have not yet learned to speak. Of course, we do speak—we rarely stop—but our speaking is not, or not yet, from the heart. If it were, we would, in the first instance, have to acknowledge and to own our own heartbreak, since, in a world such as this, our hearts too must surely be breaking, even if we screen out the terrible sound of their fracture from our own inner ears. Far from revealing ourselves to ourselves as we really are in our world and equally far from revealing the true face of the other who calls out to us even now, it seems "men speak only to conceal the mind" (Edward Young).[33]

We have seen how Heidegger interpreted language as the power of enabling us to see ourselves and our world. But most people do not perhaps fully recognize the extraordinary power of language and few will have been inducted into it in the kind of near-miraculous and unforgettable moment of vision to which Helen Keller testified. At least, few will remember it as adults. But even if that is how it was for all of us in early infancy, we have mostly long since covered over that original vision in our daily traffic with "words, words, words." This correlates with Heidegger's view that our induction into language typically has the form of participating in what he calls *Gerede*, generally translated in English as "idle talk." What is said in *Gerede* possesses an "average intelligibility," but (as opposed to the kind of revelatory discourse in which what is being talked about comes to view in what is said) the "being-with-one-another" of the talkers is allowed to take precedence over the "primary relationship-of-Being towards the entity being talked about" (BT, 169 / 212). Even when there is no deliberate intention to deceive, such talk "serves not so much to keep Being-in-the-world open for us in an articulated understanding, as rather to close it off, and cover up the entities within-the-world" (BT, 169 / 212). *Gerede* is what "one" says, what everyone says, what all of us understand. The words in which it is articulated are passed along and circulated without our stopping to attend to the extraordinary revelations of which they are capable and so we fail to hear what they could be telling us. And this can be as true of scholarly discourse as of street-corner gossip. The issue of truth, then, is not whether what is being said is conventionally true or not. It may be true to say or to write that "*Being and Time* contains important discussions of

33. Quoted in Kierkegaard, *Kierkegaard's Journals and Notebooks*, 191.

language and truth" or that "*x* is having an affair with y," but in each case the saying or writing may entirely fail to reveal what is really at issue in what is being talked about. The note-taker who has jotted down that "*Being and Time* contains important discussions of language and truth" may have very little conception of what is said in these "important" discussions or why they are important and, what is worse, the very fact of being able to repeat this may make it harder for such a note-taker to move on to the next level because s/he already "knows" what needs to be said about language and truth in *Being and Time*. Similarly, it may be true that *x* is having an affair with *y*, but passing such information on in the mode of gossip may be and, in this case, usually is a way of blocking off any deeper understanding that might want to probe why this has happened or what it means to each of the lovers or their families or colleagues. The question of truth, then, is not just whether what is said is correct, but whether it genuinely serves to uncover the matter at issue.

Heidegger's reflections on *Gerede* have often been linked to Kierkegaard's remarks about the "chatter" that the Danish writer saw as dominating the public discourse of his day, nearly a century earlier. Yet where Kierkegaard's critique of "chatter" definitely has a moral charge, aimed especially at the malice of popular journalistic literature, Heidegger is not setting out to make a moral point. He is merely saying that this is how most of us most of the time learn to speak, falling in with how everyone else is speaking and learning our words from how others use them without really attending to whether what is being said is being said in an original way. For us, in this situation, learning to speak truthfully—that is, learning to speak in such a way that what we are talking about gets revealed in how we talk about it—will be a constant struggle against the entropy of the public and private speech of our time.

In the Age of Technology

The situation of the word's original revelatory power being covered up by the prevalence of *Gerede* is further exacerbated by what Heidegger sees as a salient feature of the contemporary world: that it is on a hitherto unknown scale an "age of technology" and this, he thinks, poses a particular challenge for language. We shall come back to how this view is also reflected in Muir's analysis of the situation that "we . . . here" find ourselves in, although first it might be helpful to flag what might seem to be a major difference between

Muir and both Heidegger and Kierkegaard. Kierkegaard, for example, makes it very clear that if we are to free ourselves from the spell of "chatter" the "individual" must somehow be prized away from the crowd and spoken to as an individual. "The crowd is untruth," he insists.[34] Similarly, as we have already seen, Heidegger sees authentic speech as dependent on facing up to our being-towards-death, something that, he thinks, we can only do in utter solitude, alone with the silent voice of conscience. This, then, would seem to mark a major difference between Muir (with his insistence on the "we") and the existentialist philosophers, whatever other similarities we might find between them. Is this so? The question is important, but perhaps it is not the most important question at this point. Instead I shall turn to see what Heidegger says about the impact of the age of technology on language and how this critique has been developed by some commentators on the peculiar fate of language in our time. We shall then come back to Muir and see how such a critique relates to his own view of modern nihilism's impact on our ability to speak the needful word from the heart.

In his 1951–52 lectures *What is Called Thinking?*, Heidegger comments on the "one-sidedness" of technocratic thinking and draws attention to changes that are occurring in everyday language usage. He says

> A symptom, at first sight quite superficial, of the growing power of one-track thinking is the increase everywhere of designations consisting of abbreviations of words, or combinations of their initials. Presumably no one here has ever given serious thought to what has already come to pass when you, instead of University, simply say "Uni." "Uni"—that is like "movie." True, the moving picture theatre continues to be different from the academy of the sciences. Still, the designation "Uni" is not accidental, let alone harmless. It may even be in order for you to go in and out of the "Uni" and study "phy. sci." But the question remains what kind of order is heralded here in the spreading of this kind of language. Perhaps it is an order into which we are drawn, and to which we are abandoned, by that which withdraws from us.[35]

Heidegger's view of the implications of what he called "planetary technology" for the living, speaking voice are perhaps most succinctly summed up in a comment in the lectures *On the Essence of Language* that we today (i.e., in the 1950s) are experiencing the "thorough technicization of

---

34. Kierkegaard, *The Point of View*, 106.
35. Heidegger, *What is Called Thinking?*, 34–35 (adapted).

all languages as instruments of interplanetary information. Meta-language and Sputnik, meta-linguistics and rocket science are one and the same."[36]

A further dimension of the challenges with which this situation confronts us is highlighted by one of Heidegger's students, Hannah Arendt, when she writes:

> Wherever the relevance of speech is at stake, matters become political by definition, for speech is what makes man a political being. If we would follow the advice, so frequently urged upon us, to adjust our cultural attitudes to the present status of scientific achievement, we would in all earnest adopt a way of life in which speech is no longer meaningful. . . . [For t]he reason why it may be wise to distrust the political judgment of scientists *qua* scientists is not primarily their lack of "character" . . . but precisely the fact that they move in a world [i.e., of mathematical symbols] where speech has lost its power. And whatever men do or know or experience can make sense only to the extent that it can be spoken about. There may be truths beyond speech, and they may be of great relevance to man in the singular, that is, to man in so far as he is not a political being, whatever else he may be.[37]

Arendt's point here is not just that acronyms, abbreviations, and the general technicization of language is flattening out the rich resources of expression and invention bequeathed by the language we have inherited from the past and therefore diminishing our own lived quality of experience, but that this flattening out and functionalization of language is also corrosive of a genuine political, i.e., common life. Recalling Muir's emphasis on the "we," the search for a kind of language that would do justice to the heart is not just a matter that concerns individuals. It also concerns how we are together, as a race, a people, a "we" in the fullest and deepest sense. It is in the fullest sense of the word *political* (and nor would Wordsworth have dissented from this view and its implication that the struggle to express the true poetic word is also a struggle for the soul of society). And perhaps it is not coincidence that it was the in the same passage at the start of his *Politics* that Aristotle defined human beings as both the "beings having logos" and also as essentially "political beings."

With regard to the question concerning the relationship between language and technology, the time when Heidegger and even Arendt were

---

36. Heidegger, *Unterwegs zur Sprache*, 160.

37. Arendt, *The Human Condition*, 3–4.

writing and teaching can easily seem like another planet. Even the 1980s, prior to the advent of the internet and mobile phones, can seem positively archaic. Since then the advent of IT has saturated virtually every aspect of human interaction. It is or is rapidly becoming the universal medium in which, as communicative beings, we live and move and are, seemingly fulfilling Teilhard de Chardin's prediction of the coming noosphere, a membrane of consciousness encompassing the globe as a kind of globalized nous or mind. Nevertheless, there seem to be grounds for reserve—and one of Heidegger's central complaints against the age of technology was not to do with its objective impact on one or other aspect of our lives but on its tendency to numb our capacity for thought. It is a refrain of the lectures *What is Called Thinking?* that, in this most thought-provoking of ages, we are not yet thinking. The point, then, is not to attack or to try to get rid of technology but to be thinking in the way we are with our technology rather than simply being dazzled by it and swept off our feet into a current of thoughtless transformations, including transformations of our very own being. But if that is how it is with regard to thinking, will it not be equally or all the more demanding to hold fast to the kind of speech we might associate with the heart—the lyric moment of poetry?

The tension that is at issue here is one already inherent in the basic impulse of a Romanticism such as Wordsworth's. For the valorization of the lyric moment is there expressed precisely as a liberating counter-movement to everything involved in the rapid industrialization and urbanization of the modern world, the emergent age of technology. In the era of Romanticism itself, the tension between the purity of the speaking, singing heart and technological mediation is never more neatly stated than in Hans Christian Andersen's tale *The Nightingale*, published in the *New Tales* of 1844. Let me remind you of it. In the woods surrounding the gardens of the Emperor of China lived a nightingale, whose song would make even the hard-pressed fishermen pause in their toil. The nightingale was eventually brought to the Emperor. When it sang for him, it sang so beautifully that it brought a tear to his eye, but when the Emperor tried to reward him the nightingale answered that this tear, sprung from the Emperor's heart, was its greatest reward. Some time later, however, the Emperor receives a gift from the Emperor of Japan—an artificial nightingale that sings the same song over and over again. The Court Musician sees this as a great improvement, since, as he says, "With the real nightingale you can never calculate what is about to happen, but in the case of the artificial bird, everything is determined!"[38] The real nightingale is sent away, and its song is replaced with the artificial birdsong. But after a while the mechanism breaks and the artificial bird falls silent. When the Emperor falls ill it is unable to sing to him and relieve his suffering. He is close to death, but, at the critical moment, the song of the real nightingale is heard through the window. Death too hears it, is distracted, and the Emperor lives. The nightingale once more refuses to be rewarded, for all it wants is to come and go as it wills. It was not made to live in a palace, and it loves the Emperor's heart—and the tear sprung from his heart—more than his Crown. Its only wish is that its visits to the Emperor are kept secret from the world. Yet if Andersen's artful tale succeeds in touching our own hearts, that very motif of secrecy signals a limit to the lyric moment's power to engage, move, or change the reality of the outer world that, as Wordsworth complained "is too much with us."

This tension or, better, paradox at the heart of Romanticism's concept of poetic vocation is nicely epitomized in Walter Benjamin's description of a later, and darker poet, Charles Baudelaire, as "a lyric poet in the era of high capitalism." However, as Benjamin's study also showed, the fate of such a lyric poet was to be socially marginalized. His "song" could at best correspond to a kind of terrorism, a refusal of the reality of contemporary society that was unable materially to transform it.[39] How might a poet learn to sing in such a way as to liberate the language of the heart and to do so in such a way that it would be fruitful for the overall transformation of human social relationships?

And if such questions were already pressing in the nineteenth century, will they not be all the more urgent in an age such as ours that has been technicized to a degree unimaginable to a Wordsworth, an Andersen, a Baudelaire, or even for that matter a Heidegger or an Arendt? And will not the heart's capacity to express its truth be proportionately all the more inhibited and stifled, even to the point of annihilation? And if this is so, might there not be reasons for thinking that the humanity of humanity might itself be under threat? Some evidence that this might be so can be found in several recent studies of language and technology that emphasize what we might call the moral dimension of the challenge these technologies pose. Naomi Baron's *Always On: Language in an Online and Mobile World* and Maggie Jackson's *Distracted* are just two studies that point to a deterioration in collective capacities for attention and both agree in seeing

38. Andersen, editor, *Eventyr. II: Nye Eventyr 1844–48*, 23.

39. See Benjamin, *Charles Baudelaire*.

this as having significant moral and human implications—especially when it is a matter of attending to what actual other people are saying to us.[40] As Jackson sums up: "In this new world, something is amiss. And that something is attention."[41] But, of course, not paying attention is the perfect way to avoid the heartbreak of genuine human relationships. Attention, focus, and awareness are core values of the listening, speaking heart. And the outcome of chronic and technologically reinforced inattention may not be just a matter of a growing ocean of indifference between people, it may be something worse, what Lee Siegel, a one-time blogger for *New Republic* and by no means an instinctive opponent of electronic media, has called "the electronic mob,"[42] taking a step further the cultural decline described, a generation ago, by Christopher Lasch as the culture of narcissism and which he too saw as a culture of constant, incipient violence.[43]

Heidegger's anxieties, we recall, were focused on how the technologization of language was inhibiting our capacity for thinking. If we connect these anxieties with what was said in *Being and Time* about *Gerede* and about the call of conscience, then we can see that what is worrying him is how such technologization reinforces the *Gerede*-character of everyday language and therefore reinforces our reluctance to face up to the utterly individuating consciousness of our own finitude and mortality. I have noted that Heidegger's own view of language seemed to lack an appropriate attention to the role of the other, the *inter*-locutor, the one who by speaking to us awakens our capacity for speaking, as Anne Mansfield Sullivan did for Helen Keller. Yet seeing his critique of technicized language in connection with the concerns of more recent commentators about the impact of communication technologies on the dimension of the *inter*-personal may help us see why this is not just the reaction of an instinctive cultural conservative. In distracting us from ourselves, the technicized *Gerede* of the contemporary world increasingly distracts us from the other, as our power

40. See also Turkle, *Alone Together.*

41. Jackson, *Distracted*, 13.

42. Siegel, *Against the Machine*, 3.

43. This might seem to confirm the link Hubert Dreyfus makes between Kierkegaard's excoriation of the Danish press of the 1840s and the world of the internet. See Dreyfus, *On the Internet*, especially chapter 4. However, Siegel wants to argue that genuine journalism has essentially different values and outcomes from the blogosphere. As he puts it "A good newspaper gives you pictures of what other people are feeling. The first-person nature of blogs is like a firewall against sympathetic feelings" (Siegel, *Against the Machine*, 170).

of attention and empathy atrophy—maybe even in direct inverse propor-
tion to the extent we are "always on."[44]

None of this would have surprised Muir. For he too sees our age as
"abstract" and "impersonal" and he connects its abstract and impersonal
character both to the problem of language in general and, quite specifically
to what, in this poem, he calls heartbreak. A significant pointer to Muir's
own position is found in Hermann Broch's novel *The Sleepwalkers,* that he
and Willa (probably mostly Willa) translated immediately on its appearance
in German.[45] Broch's analysis provides a helpful and culturally specific link
between the kind of concerns we have seen in the philosophy of *Existenz*
and the world of Muir's poetry—and, like Heidegger and other more recent
thinkers, Broch connected the crisis of language in his contemporary world
with its readiness to succumb to ideologies of war and violence.

The narrative of *The Sleepwalkers* is interspersed with ten fragments of
an essay on "The Disintegration of Values." Broch sees the problem of values in the contemporary world as intertwined with the impact of the First
World War. In the world into which the war has plunged European humanity, the relationships between dream, reality, knowledge, art, society, and life
itself have become distorted to the point of a collective insanity—the point
at which a so-called Führer could motivate people to undertake actions
that, in a really real world, would be considered crazy.[46] But the roots of this
insanity lie deeper. Take the style of modern architecture, Broch suggests.
Never before has a human culture developed a style completely lacking in
ornament and this lack of ornament, this brutal functionality, he argues, is
a "writing on the wall" for the spiritual condition of the age (or "non-age,"
as he refers to it).[47] Although Broch gives architecture a certain eminence as
revelatory of the style of an age he sees each cultural product, each action,
and each thought as manifesting the common style of its age and what we

44. In this vein Gabriel Marcel, Martin Buber, Nicholas Berdyaev were all existential
thinkers who clearly emphasized the personal and interpersonal nature of essential communication and already observed the negative possibilities of modern communications
technologies for such communication.

45. The Muirs also played a role in persuading the Home Office to allow Broch, an
Austrian Jew, to be admitted to Britain in 1938, after he had suffered a period of impris-
onment. See Willa Muir, *Belonging*, 198–99.

46. Broch, *The Sleepwalkers*, 375.

47. Ibid., 391. Broch's original text uses the biblical "menetekel," thus referring
explicitly to the words written by an invisible hand on the wall at the Babylonian King
Belshazzar's feast, as described in the book of Daniel, chapter 8, and interpreted by the
prophet as a warning that Belshazzar's kingdom was about to fall.

see in the style of this present age is "our dread of nothingness, our dread of Time, which conducts us to death." This is especially salient in architecture because architecture, by virtue of its spatiality, is supremely expressive of how human beings attempt to negate time and deny its significance for their lives. Thus, he concludes, "an epoch which is completely under the dominion of death and hell must live in a style that can longer give birth to ornament."[48] This modern style is equally visible in the basic logic of values in the modern world, from the ideology of the Prussian military academy to the pragmatic, task-focused attitude of the average modern person. And behind this, as for Heidegger, are some basic metaphysical assumptions.

As Broch sees it, where we are now is the result of many centuries and even millennia of intellectual and cultural development, from the time of ancient polytheism to modern nihilism. Where the polytheistic world had manifold explanations for the various phenomena encountered by archaic human beings and each animal, each mountain, each river would have its own tutelary deity, the advent of monotheism marked an enormous simplification. Ultimately all phenomena are traceable back to one final cause: God. Even in early modernity, however, this God was still conceived in a finite, anthropomorphic form that made Him commensurable with human thought and experience. But as modernity has progressed "God" has been rendered as "a real infinity of abstraction" and so consciousness loses any sense of there being a point at which it might stop.[49] All of this process is also reflected in language itself, as it increasingly loses the style once formed by the concrete and vivid impressions of a world of immediate and real relationships and gradually reaches the point at which logic and mathematics become the gold standard of meaning.[50] The consequence of this is a ruthless focus on the aims and objectives of a given sphere of action, without regard to its relation to the whole. It is the military logic of applying force in the most consistent and radical way in order to achieve a given goal, even if this means destroying peoples, cathedrals, and hospitals. It is the logic of business that progresses ineluctably to larger and larger monopolies. It is the logic of modern painting that aims at "pure" painting, even if this is completely esoteric and no longer communicates to any but a chosen few. It is the logic of revolutions that are prepared to go all the way to dictatorship.

48. Broch, *The Sleepwalkers*, 398.

49. Ibid., 426.

50. One might note that Broch was Viennese and well aware of the role of his native city in the development of logical positivism.

"War is war," "art for art's sake," and "business is business" are comparable expressions of this goal-directed logic. As such they are also expressions of a world no longer grounded in the stability and security of a common order of Being, as was the medieval world, and cast adrift into an endless process of Becoming. Human beings who could once believe themselves to have been made in the image of God and, as such, mirroring the eternal divine values, now limit themselves to the values and functions specific to their social vocation. Religion is no longer the common ground of society but is fragmented into sects and the pursuit of arbitrary "religious experiences." The categorical imperative of duty in Protestantism has a certain severe severity or rigor but it offers no concrete or comprehensive synthesis of values that might guide the individual in deciding what "duty" actually means. And, Broch comments, there is "There is no severity that may not be a mask for fear."[51] In this case, it is anxiety in face of the unrelieved terror of an unmediated encounter with the absolute, as experienced (or so Broch suggests) by Kierkegaard.

It is indeed in Protestantism and, he says, in Judaism that this modern rigor is most apparent since both offer a religion without ornament, a religion of absolute duty and absolute law.[52] Such absolute dread deadens language itself, striking humanity dumb in face of a world stripped of value and depth. In such an age there is an increasing indifference to language, a "weariness of words."[53] Values are no longer expressive of the intentions of value-positing individuals but of abstract formulae and "reasons." But it is—or was!—precisely the grounding of values in living human individuals that grounded the possibility of mutual understanding, the translatability of languages, and the unity of humanity. Where language is truly expressive of real human life, every word—every Logos, as Broch puts it—reveals the Word of God that is the measure of all things for human beings.[54] This is why, according to Broch, absolute rational autonomy is "more 'evil' and

51. Broch, *The Sleepwalkers*, 524. The word translated here as "fear" is "angst," elsewhere translated by the Muirs as "dread."

52. He also suggests that this is connected with modern Anti-Semitism, since "the Jew" so clearly represents the direction modern society is taking and is therefore a prime target for those who react against modernity and all its works.

53. Broch, *The Sleepwalkers*, 560. Broch may be alluding here to the kind of view of the fate of language in modernity found in his fellow-Viennese Hugo von Hoffmansthal's "Letter to Lord Chandos." See Hugo von Hofmannsthal, *The Lord Chandos Letter and Other Writings*.

54. Broch, *The Sleepwalkers*, 564.

'sinful' . . . than the irrational: for, in contradistinction to the plastic irrational, the pure Ratio, arising through dialectic and deduction, becomes
set and incapable of further formation when it grows autonomous" and,
because it annihilates the possibility or validity of form-creating power, it
is "radically evil."[55] It is also, as we have seen, a result of Protestantism, a
religious vision that has produced "the unaccented vacuum of a ruthless
absoluteness, in which the abstract Spirit of God is enthroned . . . reigning
in sorrow amid the terror of dreamless, unbroken silence that constitutes
the pure [i.e., abstract, formless] Logos."[56]

But Broch is not entirely pessimistic, since he believes that no matter how far we go in the direction of the "muteness of the abstract," there
remains "the voice that binds our loneliness to all other lonelinesses, and
it is not the voice of dread and doom; it falters in the silence of the Logos
and yet is borne by it, raised over the clamour of the non-existent. It is the
voice of man and of the tribes of men, the voice of comfort and hope and
immediate love: 'Do thyself no harm! for we are all here!'"[57]

Returning to Muir we see that these kinds of concerns about the in-
tertwining of an abstract and inhuman logic with the fate of modernity and
the role of historical Protestantism in engendering this situation—as well
as the implications for poetry itself as the art of "the Word"—are especially
forcefully reflected in his poem, "The Incarnate One," which takes polemi-
cal aim at "King Calvin with his iron pen, / And God three angry letters in a
book." In such theology, he says, "the Mystery is impaled and bent / Into an
ideological instrument." But Muir's concern is not solely and perhaps not
even primarily with the theological debates of the past. Apart from what
he sees as the particularly negative effects of Calvinism on his own Scottish culture, Calvin is more generally the forerunner of a problem facing
modern European humanity: "The fleshless word, growing, will bring us
down," warns Muir, in what he predicts will be an "Abstract calamity, save
for those who can / Build their cold empire on the abstract man." Their
"bloodless word will battle for its own / Invisibly in brain and nerve and
cell."[58] And, sometimes, it seems as if they have already won. In "Song for a

---

55. Ibid., 626–7.

56. Ibid., 639–40.

57. Ibid., 648.

58. However, although the poem suggests a link between the dis-incarnation of the
word in a certain Calvinism and a certain modernity, it should be pointed out that in his
biography of John Knox, Muir rejects interpretations of Knox that make him the pro-
genitor of those features of Scottish intellectual life that would bear fruit in the Scottish

Hypothetical Age" it seems that "they" are, in fact, "we": "We, exempt from grief and rage, / Rule here our new impersonal age." *Here*—"the hot heart petrifies / And the round earth to rock is grown / In the winter of our eyes; / Heart and earth a single stone. Until the stony barrier break / Grief and joy no more shall wake."

"We . . . here," then, are those who inhabit this hypothetical, abstract, and impersonal age. Even the most powerful act we are now capable of in this nuclear age, the destruction of the world in an all-out nuclear exchange, would be no more than a "Mechanical parody of the Judgment Day / That does not judge but only deals damnation" ("The Day before the Last Day"). We are "exempt from grief and rage" but this is so far from being liberating that it merely exemplifies the extent to which—and perhaps even the reason why—our hearts have turned to stone and become incapable of speaking, which, as we have supposed, means also being incapable of listening and hearing the hearts that, even now, might be breaking. To escape such a fate, we must let our unbroken hearts be broken and, in their breaking, learn to hear the heartbreak of others so that by hearing we may learn to speak the truth of our own heart and discover our own heartbreak.

Enlightenment and, as Froude had argued, "steam-engines and railroads." See Muir, *John Knox*, 304f.

III

Time, teach us the art
That breaks and heals the heart.

Time and Essential Loss

The last two lines of verse one introduce a new topic: time. It is a topic that will by no means be new to readers of Muir's poetry, in which the riddle, terror, and, ultimately, the gift of time is a constant theme. His longest poem, published as a separate volume, was entitled *Variations on a Time Theme*, but this is only one of many examples. Central to Muir's fascination with time was the challenge posed by Nietzsche's doctrine of eternal recurrence, a teaching that Nietzsche himself spoke of as unfathomable and terrifying and one that commentators have remained deeply divided about. As an example of how the Nietzschean terror of time is figured in Muir's poetry, we might turn to the second section of *Variations on a Time Theme*, where he depicts life as a journey across a "boundless plain" on which we are carried by horses that, like heraldic figures, have made the same journey, generation after generation, always the same, indifferent to their riders and never reaching the goal: "Time has such curious stretches, we are told, / And generation after generation / May travel them, sad stationary journey, / Of what device, what meaning?" But the challenge is most forcefully and directly stated in the seventh section of Variations:

> Ransomed from darkness and released in Time,
> Caught, pinioned, blinded, sealed and cased in Time,
> Summoned, elected, armed and crowned by Time,
> Tried and condemned, stripped and disowned by Time;
> Suckled and weaned, plumped and full-fed by Time,
> Defrauded, starved, physicked and bled by Time;
> Buried alive and buried dead by Time:
> If there's no crack or chink, no escape from Time . . .
> Nothing in heaven or earth to set us free:
> Imprisonment's for ever; we're the mock of Time,
> While lost and empty lies Eternity.

"The Recurrence" explicitly addresses Nietzsche as teacher of this dread doctrine, with its message that even eternity "Cannot cancel, cannot add / One to your delights or tears, / Or a million million years / Tear the nightmare from the mad." Each of us in a universe of infinitely recurring time "will miss / Achievement by the self-same inch." As in "The Journey Back," our life's journey is experienced both as infinitely remote from the starting place and lived in expectation of a harvest that will never come.

This is not all Muir has to say about time. Already in "The heart could never speak" we are hearing another variation on the time theme, since time is now being addressed as a teacher, as one who can teach us the art that breaks and heals the heart. And this, as we have learned in considering the fate of the heart in the abstract and impersonal age of technology, is a teaching we need to learn if we are to remain or fully to become creatures capable of speaking with one another from the heart. But before we return to how Muir's understanding of time is not exhausted in the vision of eternal recurrence, let us sketch something of the philosophical and religious background of the topic so as to see the extent to which his struggle with time relates to the wider intellectual and cultural interpretation of this universal phenomenon.

Muir, and Nietzsche before him, did not address time simply as a concept or problem in physics; that is, time as measured and defined by cosmological principles. Rather, both attempted to figure and understand time in terms of our human experience of it. Both were furthermore attentive to a long tradition of interpretation that sees time as essentially destructive of all that is of value in human life. Already Psalm 103 declares that "the days of man are but as grass; he flourishes like a flower of the field: when the wind blows over it, it is gone and its place will know it no more" or, as the once popular hymn had it "Time like an ever-rolling stream / bears all his sons away." That we are creatures of time means that we are exposed to constant change, chance, and contingency and that, from the very beginning, our lives are, as it were, thrown towards their final dissolution in death. The point was, once more, eloquently stated by Augustine:

> Wherever man's soul may turn, it only encounters suffering if it settles anywhere but in you [i.e. God], even if it is to attach itself to beautiful things outside of you and of itself; for there would be nothing if they were not by you; they appear and disappear; their advent is like a beginning of being, they grow to perfect it and once this perfection is attained, they come apart in old age and in death and all of them do not reach old age, but all go towards death. For

when they appear and lead to being, the faster they grow to get there, the faster also they rush into nothingness.[59]

Perhaps even more vivid is Hölderlin's image of existence as a waterfall in the poem "Hyperion's Song of Fate," an image that is visually enhanced by its flowing structure on the page:

> Doch uns ist gegeben,
>> Auf keiner Stätte zu ruhn,
>> Es schwinden, es fallen
>> Die leidenden Menschen
>> Blindlings von einer
>> Stunde zur andern,
>> Wie wasser von Klippe
>> Zu Klippe geworfen,
>> Jahrlang ins Ungewisse hinab.[60]

Indeed, in "Hölderlin's Journey" Muir portrays the German poet as himself a victim of time's illusions, setting out on the journey to Bordeaux to seek his beloved muse, his "Diotima," who has, in fact, died before he even set out: "For now I know / Diotima was dead / Before I left the starting place; Empty the course, the garland gone, / And all that race as motionless / As these two heads of stone." As in "The Journey Back" it is revealed that there is no "prize" to be won, no goal to be attained in time's endless expanse—a discovery that is here seen as the occasion of Hölderlin's descent into the madness of his last years.

What this view of time as extended between an infinite past and an infinite future shares with Nietzsche's teaching on eternal recurrence is that it robs us of the possibility of any decisive action. Nothing, in the long run, makes any difference; nothing is ever gained or secured. Whatever is done will be undone and, doubtless, done again, equally meaninglessly. Even if it does not literally "all come round again" it is a situation in which, as Nietzsche put it in a late fragment on nihilism, "Existence has no goal or end; any comprehensive unity in the plurality of events is lacking: the character of existence is not 'true,' is *false*. . . . Briefly: the categories 'aim,' 'unity,'

---

59. Augustine, *Confessions* 4.10. Translated by Emilie zum Brunn in *St. Augustine: Being and Nothingness*, 2–3.

60. Translation: Yet to us is not given to find any place to rest; suffering humanity evanesces and falls blindly from one hour into the next—like water tossed from rock to rock, year after year down into uncertainty.

'being,' which we used to project some value into the world—we *pull out* again; so the world looks *valueless.*"[61]

It is such a depiction of time that provides one of the basic impulses behind *Being and Time*. There, as Heidegger makes clear in the early pages, "Being" is not construed as an object we have to track down and define: instead, what the enquiry is about is the *meaning* of Being. But the problem for the modern world is that whereas Augustine—whose sense for the impermanence of all things temporal was second to none—was able to oppose an unchanging world of selfsame, immutable divine Being to the self-annihilating world of mutable entities, that possibility has been annihilated in a world that sees itself as having experienced the death of God. In this regard it is telling that Nietzsche's madman opens his proclamation of the death of God precisely by pointing to the directionless and purposeless nature of the world left by God's decease, a world that is nothing but endless self-consuming transience:

> "Where is God gone?" he called out. "I mean to tell you! *We have killed him,*—you and I! We are all his murderers! But how have we done it? How were we able to drink up the sea? Who gave us the sponge to wipe away the whole horizon? What did we do when we loosened this earth from its sun? Wither does it now move? Wither do we move? Away from all suns? Do we not dash on unceasingly? Backwards, sideways, forwards, in all directions? Is there still an above and below? Do we not stray, as through infinite nothingness?"[62]

But if the world is nothing but time, how can "Being"—how can the fact of our existence—*mean* anything at all, ever?

In his own terms Heidegger describes this situation in terms of Dasein's "thrownness"; that is, that it comes to self-awareness as having been thrown into the world and thrown, inescapably, towards its own death (as in "Hyperion's Song of Fate"). Our coming to be was neither a result of our own choice nor is it anything explicable in terms of a sequence of natural causes. Of course, Heidegger and the other existential philosophers well understood that it is perfectly possible to give a very extensive account of the human being in terms of biological, psychological, and sociological explanations. In a certain perspective the human being is a natural phenomenon like any other and can be explained like any other. But what such

---

61. Nietzsche, *The Will to Power*, 13.
62. Nietzsche, *The Joyful Wisdom*, 168.

explanations never catch is our lived sense of being a self, what Heidegger calls the "mineness" of existence. It is precisely this that he therefore takes as the starting-point of his search for meaning in Being, even though Being (for "we moderns") is bounded on every side by infinite and endless time. Christians and others might well take issue with this analysis, arguing that time itself is bounded and limited by the eternity of God. In this connection it is striking that one of Heidegger's early colleagues, Edith Stein, writing as a Catholic convert, produced a work entitled *Finite and Eternal Being*, deliberately contesting Heidegger's view that time provided the horizon for interpreting any possible mental phenomenon—including eternity. And we also recall Muir's lament at the end of the seventh section of *Variations on a Time Theme* that, in a world in which time is everything, eternity lies "empty and lost."

It is not to my purpose here to argue for the philosophical superiority of one or other of these positions—the Nietzschean, the Heideggerian, or the Christian/metaphysical. What is important to hold on to is how, for Muir, the vertiginous vistas of a post-Nietzschean feeling for time's "infinite nothingness" presented a challenge that had to be faced. And, as he understood, the challenge is not, in the first instance, intellectual or theoretical or even poetic but *existential*. That is, it is a matter of how we experience ourselves and our own situation in the world or, to put it in first person terms, how I feel about being me, about the "I" that I am, finding myself "thrown" towards death, cast into infinite nothingness.

But there is more to realizing the utter transitoriness of human life on earth than waking up to the fact that I myself will one day die and that this unique center of consciousness I call myself will cease to be the center of its world. Time doesn't just confront us with our individual mortality, but with the unsettling of all our essential relationships—even before we ourselves "go into the dark." This further aspect of human transience has been nicely summarized by the young Israeli scholar Sharon Krishek. "Being finite and subject to the passage of time, our existence is pervaded by constant loss," she writes. "Time goes by and seems to take with it everything that gives meaning to our life. Most often this loss is quiet and inconspicuous, but at the same time it is unstoppable."[63] At any given time we will find ourselves dealing with very particular losses (what Krishek calls "actual losses"), such as moving away from a much-loved home, the death of a parent, or the break-up of a relationship, but we usually manage to console ourselves with

63. Krishek, *Kierkegaard on Faith and Love*, 10.

the thought that we nevertheless still have other good things in our lives: the new home we are moving into, the children with whose welfare we have been entrusted, the possibility of new loves and new friendships. However, as Krishek points out, none of these things are insured against loss of one kind or another. One day we will move out of the new home, one day the children will leave home and perhaps, like the prodigal son, turn their backs on us, and perhaps we will one day be separated from our new friends and lovers by disagreements, indifference, or death. Even when we are not conscious of any actual losses, then, our lives are conditioned in every respect by potential loss, and it is this constant situation of being encompassed by potential loss that Krishek calls the "essential loss" that she sees as a defining feature of human existence: "everything that we have, everything that we take to be ours, is in truth *essentially* lost to us," she writes.[64]

What could better describe how our basic experience of time is also, inevitably, an experience leading to heartbreak? Whose heart will not break, at one time or another, when life is marked by "essential loss"?

In the previous section we considered how our modern technological society protects us from hearing the word that speaks out the world's heartbreak (our own and that of others). It also protects or promises to protect us from the very experience of loss. In *Being and Time*, Heidegger described how the way in which people mostly talk about death effectively conceals the real shock of mortality. In our average everyday way of living and talking about ourselves, death is simply one event or happenstance amongst others, "a mishap which is constantly occurring—as a 'case of death.' Someone or other dies, be he neighbour or stranger. . . . 'One of these days one will die too, in the end; but right now it has nothing to do with us.'" (BT, 253–54 / 296–97). In keeping with the general characteristics of "idle talk," death is so far from being a unique, all-encompassing event that it is spoken about as an event or occurrence like any other, something that has no definite meaning but is swathed in ambiguity, and, above all, something that always happens only to "one," not to *me*: "In Dasein's public way of interpreting, it is said that 'one dies,' because everyone else and oneself can talk himself into saying that 'in no case is it I myself,' for this 'one' is the 'nobody'" (BT, 253 / 297). Even in dealing with those who are dying, we assure them that it'll be alright and that things will soon return to normal: "In this manner the 'they' provides a constant tranquillization about death. At bottom, however, this is a tranquillization not only for him who is 'dying'

64. Ibid., 11.

but just as much for those who 'console' him" (BT, 254 / 298). If we are in any doubt about the kind of thing Heidegger is talking about, he refers us to Tolstoy's *Ivan Ilych*. We can never really experience the death of others and the possibility of doing so is constantly pre-empted by the distracting, tranquillizing ways in which "one" talks about it.

Such a tranquillization of death is especially evident in the culture of medically managed death that has grown up since the Second World War. Where it was once regarded as desirable to be able to prepare oneself for death, to speak and pray about it with one's minister or priest, and to die surrounded by one's family, today's good death is either so sudden that the dying person knows nothing about it or is pharmaceutically managed so that he or she "dies" by passing through successive stages of unconsciousness in such a way that life gradually blurs into death. At the same time, medical progress promises ever-longer postponements of the inevitable. In what is called the Methuselah project there is even excited talk of extending human life up towards a thousand years within two or three generations. But both the normalization of a way of talking about death that reduces it to a medical "problem" to be "managed" and the empty rhetoric of the Methuselah project might be taken as exemplary cases of the blending of *Gerede* and the state of constant communicational distraction that typifies our age of technology. Neither allows the true human meaning of what is at issue in death to come to expression in an adequate way.

Of course, the "ideal death" of the past was often a death of excruciating agony (Ivan Ilych's death is a case in point) and most of us are grateful that illnesses that would significantly shorten life just a few years ago can now be treated in one way or another. But in regarding aging and dying as problems to be solved—one more scientific project—we are in danger not only of misdiagnosing the human condition but of failing to see that, come what may, we cannot escape essential loss by such stratagems, merely evade it.[65]

Muir's poem "The Absent" not only provides his clearest statement of this situation of essential loss, but is arguably one of the most precise statements on the subject available to us. In the poem he reverses our normal

65. Of course, nothing that has been said here should be taken as constituting an argument for withholding available medicines or for not developing new treatments. The question is more about what we think we're doing and what we hope to achieve through such means, as well as a reminder that they conspicuously do not answer the challenge as to how we and the dying are to *talk* to one another so as to allow the event of dying to be a maximally human event; that is, an event in life and not merely a matter of decease.

assumptions about loss. It is not they, "the absent" of the title, who are the others, but we, who, in their absence, are "the others": "And we, we are the Others / Who walk by ourselves unquestioned in the sun / Which shines for us and only for us. / For they are not here." "And so," he concludes, "we sorrow for These that are not with us, / Not knowing that we sorrow or that this is our sorrow, / Since it is long past thought or memory or device of mourning, / Sorrow for loss of that which we never possessed, / The unknown, the nameless . . ." Grieving, we do not know that we grieve, we miss seeing what—or better "those"—we miss and have always missed. The human condition, in other words, is a condition of chronic mourning, albeit we strive continually and often very successfully to avoid thinking of it in these terms. To do so would be to expose our superficially "unbroken" hearts to the deep heartbreak of existence.

We shall return to further aspects of this situation of essential loss in our meditation on verse 2 of "The heart could never speak" and the explicit naming of the dead that occurs there. The point here is simply to underline and to characterize further the implications of the essential loss that we constantly live with by virtue of our living in time and to show how this situation is also essentially one of heartbreak—whether we hear that heartbreak or whether we have already set up our defenses against ever having to listen to it.

But if time can in this way teach us the heartbreak, why does Muir speak of this as an "art," and how might time also teach us the art "that heals the heart"?

Certainly I do not think we should read "art" here as something purely "aesthetic" nor even as a skill like the "art of cooking" or the so-called "art of living." But why do we need "art" at all in this case? Surely the kinds of experiences we have been thinking about—the actual losses that constantly accompany us and remind us of our situation of essential loss—are sufficiently powerful to break our hearts whether we will or no. Krishek began her analysis with Augustine's justly famous account of his own uncontrollable grief at the death of a close friend. Surely this anecdote illustrates that in the face of real, actual loss grief is mostly all too uncontrollable. Surely there is no art in this. We don't have to learn how to grieve. It happens. Even if we think less dramatically of the loss involved in leaving an old home or the end of a relationship, we are only too prone to feel the pain of such events and maybe, in this sentimental age, to wallow in it a little bit too easily. So one might think, but, as Heidegger pointed out in his account of how we tranquillize ourselves against the prospect of death, our way of feeling and showing our pain is very often and perhaps very naturally to ignore it, to deny it, or somehow or other to minimize it, to choke back the tears and get on with life. Even our ritualized expressions of shock, horror, and grief, no matter how histrionic (and perhaps most of all when they are most histrionic) are also means of avoidance: how often do such phrases as "I'm really gutted" or "You're breaking my heart" or "I really feel for you" actually carry the force the words suggest? Often they're the easiest words of all to say. In this sense, then, letting our hearts be broken, as opposed to following our natural impulses of denial and flight, may indeed be an "art"—but, note, we have no "teacher" in this art except for time and the loss that time always and constantly brings. There is no extra knowledge, no extra equipment we need acquire before we can learn it. We just have to attend to what time is doing with us.

But that is not all. The poem also seems to suggest that time is not simply a teacher of heartbreak: it can also be a teacher in the art of healing that very same heartbreak. How can the same power that breaks our hearts be the same power that heals them? Muir himself never explicitly endorses Hölderlin's lines "Where danger is, there grows the saving power," but the thought is very much akin to many elements in his poetic vision.[66] Certainly they are lines that many other critics of the crisis of modernity took to heart, including both Heidegger and C. G. Jung. Such words may seem surprising at first, but in the light of what we have already pondered about the connection between being able to hear the heartbreak of others and becoming aware of our own heartbreak, we can see something of the homeopathic logic at work here.

In teaching us heartbreak and thus, in a sense, "growing" our capacity for having a heart and for speaking from the heart, time reveals something about itself that the teachings of eternal recurrence and of our experience of time as thrownness towards death are not able to grasp. In the poem "The Recurrence" Muir sets out Nietzsche's doctrine that "All things return" in poetic form. Having done this, he then offers a response that is spoken precisely in the name of the heart: "But the heart makes reply: / This is only what the eye / From its tower on the turning field / Sees and sees and cannot tell why . . ."[67] The "turning field," as Muir goes on to suggest, is the world of

66. Although he discusses them in two essays in his *Essays on Literature and Society*, e.g., on pp. 94–95.

67. The association of knowing and seeing with heart and head respectively is also

a "heraldic show," the world he figured in *Variations on a Time Theme* as the endlessly repeated journey of heraldic horses across a "boundless plain." Although the riders may change from one generation to another, the same journey is repeated over and over again. In such a world what happens in time has no ultimate significance. But that is just what is untrue about it, since what heartbreak teaches us is that what happens in time does have great significance.

And it is not only our own private heartbreak that teaches this. If the heraldic show is all there is, "the Actor on the Tree / Would loll at ease, miming pain, / And counterfeit mortality." The reference to Christ and to the cross (often spoken of as "the Tree") is unmistakable, and we are again reminded that such a "One" is fully incarnated and does not (and cannot) merely "counterfeit mortality" but must truly die.

"The heart," we remember, "could never speak / But that the Word was spoken." Yet, as we have seen, the ability to speak the word (understanding this in a purely human sense) is itself dependent, firstly, on our being spoken to and, secondly, on our being willing and able to attend to—really to listen to and to take to heart—the heartbreak of others. In the mutual listening and in the attentive speech that passes between two hearts conscious of each other's heartbreak, an initial and proximate relief is achieved. That our hearts learn, through heartbreak, to speak is therefore already the beginning of healing. So it is that time begins—and what teaching process ever reaches its end?—to teach us not only heartbreak but also heart-healing. Of course, if we then go a step further and understand "the Word" as referring also to the divine Word, the Word made flesh—who also, in Christian doctrine, is the coming judge of all the world, "the golden harvester" we sometimes glimpse against the evening sky—then, we might suppose, the healing that He would bestow would be deeper, more radical, and more encompassing than any healing we can bestow on each other through the mutual attention of our hearts. Then, it might be a healing that we could also call "salvation." And, as we have just seen, this salvation would, in its inner essence, be inseparable from the reality of the Word having been made flesh to the point of suffering and dying, as all flesh must suffer and die. Yet that this act of suffering and dying is the suffering and dying of "the Word" makes it a hinge on which the infinite nothingness of endlessly recurrent and infinitely empty time becomes transformed into the exchanges of love that are the language of the heart.

---

made in the poem "Head and Heart."

Verse Two

I

Heart, you would be dumb
But that your word was said
In time, and the echoes come
Thronging from the dead.

Speaking in Time

Verse 1 was composed of three two-line sentences. The first two of these offered seemingly simple statements relating to the heart's ability to speak and our ability (or inability) to hear the heart break. The third was phrased as a request to time to become our teacher in "the art that breaks and heals our heart." Verse 2 varies this pattern slightly. The first four lines compose a single sentence, somewhat (though not much) more complex than the simple statements of verse 1, but it too ends in a request to time that is also a request that time might become our teacher—only on this occasion the poet asks time to be a teacher in "the art that resurrects the heart." But before we can consider how this closing petition relates to the art "that breaks and heals the heart"—whether it is a deepening or higher level of that art or whether it is something significantly new—we have first to consider the lines that precede it.

Perhaps more significant than the fact that the first four lines of this verse form a single sentence is that the heart is now directly addressed and not merely spoken about. Whereas verse 1 began by telling us the important truth that "The heart could never speak / But that the Word was spoken," it is the heart itself that is now spoken to: "Heart, you would be dumb . . ." This seems to mark significant progress, for how could the heart be spoken to if it was deemed incapable of hearing—which, remembering what we have learned from verse 1, means that it is also a heart that has become or is becoming capable of speaking. However, it also seems that the heart being spoken to is still, as it were, a novice in the art of speaking its word. It still has much to learn, not least that its word will need to be spoken in time.

This is understandable. We have already seen why the heart might hesitate to commit itself to time and to speaking its word in time, since to do so would be to commit itself to the prospect of essential loss. Those whose words are spoken in time will certainly have their hearts broken and even if a promise of heart-healing is held out to them, the certainty of heartbreak will in many cases weigh more heavily than the possibility of heart-healing. In such a situation it might be tempting to propose to ourselves that we might be able to speak a word that would somehow be immune from the ravages of time; a word that would, as it were, reach beyond time, referring to simple, incorruptible, and eternal truths. Such is a certain form of Platonism: the notion that our words become true when they are interpreted by reference to a world of timeless ideas or truths.

Muir is not unmoved by such a possibility. In another of the posthumously published poems he writes: "And now that time grows shorter, I perceive / That Plato's is the truest poetry, / And that these shadows / Are cast by the true" (from "I have been taught"). But what might this mean in his poetic universe? In an important interlude in "The Labyrinth" he speaks of how he could not endure life in the labyrinth of eternal recurrence if he was not sustained by the conviction that it was essentially illusory. "It is a world, perhaps: but there's another," he comments.

> For once in a dream or trance I saw the gods
> Each sitting on the top of his mountain-isle,
> While down below the little ships sailed by,
> Toy multitudes swarmed in the harbours, shepherds drove
> Their tiny flocks to the pastures, marriage feasts
> Went on below, small birthdays and holidays,
> Ploughing and harvesting and life and death,
> And all permissible, all acceptable,
> Clear and secure as in a limpid dream.
> But they, the gods, as large and bright as clouds,

> Conversed across the sounds in tranquil voices
> High in the sky above the untroubled sea,
> And their eternal dialogue was peace
> Where all these things were woven, and this our life
> Was as a chord deep in that dialogue,
> As easy utterance of harmonious words,
> Spontaneous syllables bodying forth a world.
> That was the real world; I have touched it once,
> And now shall know it always.

In this vision of a life whose rhythms are held and balanced in the eternal tranquillity of a divine discourse there is, it is true, a kind of time. It is not a lifeless or motionless world. Ships go to and fro across the seas, the earth is farmed, and men and women love, marry, rear families, and die. Yet this is a simple, cyclical time; the cyclical time of agrarian societies governed by the stable order of "seed time and harvest, cold and heat, summer and winter, day and night" (Gen 8:22). At the same time, it seems to be protected against the terror of eternal recurrence. Its time is not empty or meaningless. It does not stretch out into an infinite nothingness behind and before but is encompassed by the "eternal dialogue" of the gods. It seems to be a world that has never known or has forgotten the fall into open, terrifying, historical time. As such, it may be "the real world," but is it a world we can inhabit, "*we . . . here*"?

In "The Journey back" (from the same collection as "The Labyrinth"), the self that journeys back into its own archaic past comes at one point to a similar vision of a world ordered by immortals living in unbroken blessedness.

> They walk high in their mountainland in light
> On winding roads by many a grassy mound
> And paths that wander for their own delight.
> There they like planets pace their tranquil round
> That has no end, whose end is everywhere,
> And tread as to a music underground . . . (6, 1–6).

This is an order of temporal movement higher than or at least other than that of historical time. It depicts time as a blessed dance, tranquilly progressing through a measured sequence of changes that involve no essential break in the luminous silence of the ritual-like movement. But, the poet adds, "This is the other road, not that we know" (6, 12).

Perhaps we will, one day, come to such a place and see the real or true world stripped of the shadows that, for now, obscure our vision. But while we are in time it is a vision on the very boundary of our existential possibilities, like the vision of the golden harvester in the evening light, portending a harvest that, in time, never arrives. The way to it is "the other road, not that we know." It is like our road in that it has no end, but unlike our road in that its end is "everywhere" and in such a way that, wherever one may be on this other road, the end will always already have arrived.

The time of such a world, then, is not the time in which the heart must speak and be spoken to. Our time is the time in which and by which we are thrown beyond ourselves towards the experience of "essential loss," and the first thing that confronts us on such a road is the encounter with all that we have already and irrevocably lost. As soon as the word is spoken in time, then, it is no surprise that "the echoes come / Thronging from the dead." But what is our relation to the dead? What could it possibly be?

Amongst the Dead

We have already noted Heidegger's view that the way in which we collectively talk about death is mostly such as to tranquillize what might be our otherwise uncontrollable fear and anxiety in the face of annihilation. Part of the trick of such tranquillizing talk is to speak about death as if it is just something happening, and especially something happening to someone else, somewhere else, sometime else. According to Heidegger, we cannot experience the death of others, and therefore to speak about death always and only as if it was something that concerned others is a highly effective way of marginalizing the awareness that our being is a being-towards-death. In the strictest terms, I only really confront death when I confront it as my own death. But a further implication of this is that with regard to my own, unique experience of being thrown towards death, "the dead" have no essential relation to me. They are also amongst the others whose deaths I experience merely as a kind of fact amongst other facts (no matter how distressing). In dying the other undergoes "that remarkable phenomenon of Being which may be defined as the change-over of an entity from Dasein's kind of Being (or life) to no-longer-Dasein. The end of the entity qua Dasein is the beginning of the same entity qua something present-at-hand"

(BT, 238 / 281). This doesn't mean that the dead have simply become objects like any others, and Heidegger suggests that the corpse about to be dissected by a medical student is still an object of a different kind from, for example, a piece of wood about to be planed down by a carpenter. The dead will always be those who have ceased to live, who were once alive. Even though they no longer have any possibility for being with us, we still have the possibility of being with them, as in what Heidegger calls "a mode of respectful solicitude" (BT, 238 / 282)—or, as we might gloss Heidegger's words, the possibility of "loving memory."

But what Muir is saying here seems to be something different. For Muir, the first thing we hear when we speak our word in time are "the echoes" that "come thronging from the dead." There is, it seems, an intimate connection between, on the one hand, the heart learning to speak and, on the other, the experience of essential loss that is figured in hearing the echoes that come thronging from the dead. Whereas for Heidegger the truth of my "ownmost" relation to my ineluctably solitary death is to be found only in just this quality of exclusive mineness, Muir seems to figure the discovery of our own heart—the core of our inner self-identity—as essentially bound up with our relation to the dead, "the others." But in what way "bound up"?

We have already several times touched on the poem "The Journey Back," in which Muir undertakes a journey back through the sedimented layers of his psychic existence, setting out (as he puts it) to "Seek the beginnings, learn from whence you came, / And know the various earth of which you are made." This takes him through the embedded memories of his father's world and back to an archaic, prehistoric world. So too in "The Fathers" where he connects the "panics and furies" that torment us in the present to the "archaic fevers" originating in "The fathers' anger and ache" that "Will not, will not away / And leave the living alone."

Muir underwent intense psycho-analysis for a period and such poems can be connected to the analytic process and the uncovering of the primitive psychic life that lives on in the conscious present of the individual. But there is more to such an inner journey back than simply tracking the aetiology of one or other current neurosis. I have referred to Muir's "socialism" and an important aspect of that is to do with his sense of solidarity with the many generations of poor Orkney farmers from whom he was descended. The ancient dead are remembered not merely in filial duty, as in a form of "respectful solicitude," nor yet that they might be exorcised and leave the present self free to pursue its autonomous devices. For Muir the self is what it is as a part of and in solidarity with the larger human community, the tribe, the people, "all we" (as the opening words of one poem have it). It did not choose this history or this descent, but it is an essential element in its journey to itself that it learns its identity with all who have gone before.

In the first section of *Variations on a Time Theme*, Muir poses a series of questions on behalf—once more—of a "we," a "we" that is figured as having reached a point of middle-aged indifference to life, a kind of convalescent self, "waiting for life, / Turning away from hope, too dull for speculation." So, he asks, "How did we come here . . . Where did the road branch? / Where did the path turn . . . Or did we choose . . . Did we come here through darkness or inexplicable light / Was it truth that lured us here, or falsehood? Virtue itself / Or weakness . . . ?" It is, we may say, a powerful exposition of what Heidegger calls Dasein's sense of "thrownness," of having been thrown into a world that it neither designed nor chose and also, as we have seen several times, a world it is fated to lose, thrown as it is towards its own ultimate annihilation in death. But—here we are! So who are we, and what are we to do here? "Can we build a house here," Muir asks; "Can we sing our songs here, / Pray, lift a shrine to some god?" The question is left unanswered, but is followed by a further specification of who the "we" he is talking about are. "We," he says, are "nameless," "between the impotent dead / And the unborn, cut off from both, fateless, / Yet ruled by fate." Implicit here, I suggest, is the following thought: that we ourselves will be nameless, unable, as he puts it, to "till these nameless fields," sing our songs, worship our gods, or build our houses, until we cease to be cut off from the "impotent dead / And the unborn," that is, until we understand ourselves in our deepest solidarity and identity with all our race.

"The Child Dying," written after an accident that Muir believed was going to be fatal for his son Gavin, underlines the point that the terror of death is not simply the terror of annihilation, but the breaking of all relationship between the dead and the living. The words of the poem are spoken as if by the dying child, terrified by the onset of "nothing-filled eternity." Seeking his father's hand he concludes:

> Hold my hand, oh hold it fast—
> I am changing!—until at last
> My hand in yours no more will change,
> Though your change on. You here, I there,
> So hand in hand, twin-leafed despair—
> I did not know death was so strange.

This "strangeness" has precisely to do with the separation between the living and the dead in which the dying are annihilated and the living become "the others," as in the poem "The Absent." The lives of these "others" are, we recall, permeated by a "great absence." They are unable even to mourn since they do not know for whom they might mourn, and they must consequently experience themselves as well as the absent as "nameless": "And so we sorrow for These that are not with us, / Not knowing we sorrow or that this is our sorrow . . . Sorrow for loss of that which we never possessed, / The unknown, the nameless . . ." They are incapable of being the selves that they are, i.e., unable to call themselves by their true names (speak their hearts' truth!), until they are able to sorrow, "that sorrow / And loneliness might bring a blessing upon us."

The solidarity and community of the living and the dead seems, then, to offer a rather dramatic alternative to Heidegger's view that we attain authentic existence only by turning towards our own death in full and resolute consciousness that no one else can go into the dark valley on our behalf. Such a view implies that our relation to those who have already passed that way will not finally be decisive for our own constitution as selves. Gabriel Marcel, a Catholic philosopher contemporary with Heidegger, already judged this view to be a weak point in Heidegger's analysis of Dasein, suggesting that "the consideration of one's own death is surpassed by the consideration of the death of a loved one."[1] Muir would agree but would also go further, claiming, it seems, that it is only when we remake the bonds of love undone by death that we can find a ground on which to learn our own names and to speak our heart's own truth. It is perhaps for this reason that the two poems dedicated to dead friends—"To J. F. H." and "For Ann Scott-Moncrieff"—are both addressed in the second person to their dedicatees. Dead, they still belong among the living, to be spoken to and even listened to—"Yet 'the world is a pleasant place' / I can hear your voice repeat, / While the summer shone in your face / Last summer in Princes Street."

When it is said that the heart that speaks its word in time will be answered by "echoes" that "come thronging from the dead," such moments will not be moments of passing whimsy but the revelation of a constant state of being, a new and radical orientation of the self towards the world, towards others, and towards itself. For in such moments the past is, as it were, not past, the dead are, as it were alive, and the absent are, as it were present (as Muir says to Ann Scott-Moncrieff, she is "Absent and present so

1. Marcel, *Tragic Wisdom*, 131.

much / Since out of the world you fell . . ."). "We are all here," as Broch summarized the central affirmation of authentic speech.[2] We do not remember the dead: we remember the living. Or: we remember the dead living.

There is probably no argument that might protect what has been said here from being taken as mere wish-fulfilment, mere self-indulgent and self-deluding "memory," although poets and analysands are likely to experience memory as anything but "mere" and even to find its deliverances more powerful than the evidence of what Heidegger called the average everydayness of existing as one of the crowd. In the Christian perspective, it might be seen as illustrative of the doctrine of the communion of saints, "the mystical Body of Christ, that is the blessed company of all faithful people," although in Muir's vision it is not a company that seems to be limited by subscription to a particular creed. On the contrary, as we have seen, it embraces also the long lineage of fathers and fathers' fathers who lived lives of hard and bitter struggle that often warped or broke their personalities. And this line reaches far back into pre-Christian and even prehistoric time.

"The Transfiguration" describes a momentary glimpse of "the clear unfallen world" and, as such, might be compared with the vision of life as a chord resonating within the "eternal dialogue" of the gods that we saw in the reconciling vision of "The Labyrinth." In that case, however, I suggested that the tranquil timelessness of such a vision was, as Muir put it in "The Journey Back," not our road, not the road we know. For our road is a road not only through time but through fallen time, a "winter way," as he puts it in "One Foot in Eden," leading through "famished field" and past "blackened tree." To put it otherwise, the ordered and harmonious world revealed in the vision of "The Labyrinth" is a pagan vision, a "golden age." But what we see in "The Transfiguration" is something more than an ordered and harmonious world. It is a world seen as it would be seen if we took to heart Christ's injunction that "To the pure all things are pure." In such a transfigured world it is not only the passage of trade or the tilling of the soil that find their place, but "lurkers under doorways, murderers, / With rags tied round their feet for silence, came / Out of themselves and were with us, / And those who hide within the labyrinth / Of their own loneliness and greatness came / And those entangled in their own devices, / The silent and the garrulous liars . . ." This is not simply the advent or the revelation of a deep order undergirding the apparent disorder of the world, it is the advent and the revelation of a new world, a redeemed world.

2. See above, p. 38.

If, with regard to the dead, it is a kind of memory that is in play here, it is perhaps what the Russian religious philosopher Nicholas Berdyaev called "creative memory":

> Memory of the past is spiritual; it conquers historical time. This . . . [is] a creatively transfiguring memory. It carries forward into eternal life not that which is dead in the past but what is alive, not that which is static in the past but what is dynamic. This spiritual memory reminds man, engulfed in his historical time, that in the past there have been great creative movements of the spirit and that they ought to inherit eternity. It reminds him also of the fact that in the past there lived concrete beings, living personalities, with whom we ought in existential time to have a link no less than with those who are living now. Society is always a society not only of the living but also of the dead; and this memory of the dead . . . is a creative dynamic memory. The last word belongs not to death but to resurrection. But resurrection is not a restoration of the past in its evil and untruth, but transfiguration.[3]

For Muir (as I think also for Berdyaev and Marcel) the fruits of such memory are not simple "echoes," but more—they are voices recalling us to a dialogue of love in which and through which we cease to be nameless wanderers in a nameless land and become a people, named, known, and potentially loved. This is how our hearts, once they begin to speak, must grow.

---

3. Berdyaev, *Slavery and Freedom*, 111.

II

Time, teach us the art
That resurrects the heart.

Resurrection?

Verse 2 ends in a manner very similar to verse 1. Here too, time is addressed and asked to become our teacher, this time a teacher in "the art / That resurrects the heart." Again it may seem odd to think of what is being asked for as an "art." Certainly we are now in a position to see that it is not something that is likely to come easily or naturally to us. Most of the time we are content or at least resigned to being "the others," going through life unaware of the great sorrow by which we are encompassed. And this, as we have seen, is something more than Heidegger's idea of being-towards-death and the prospective loss of ourselves and our whole world in our singular deaths, "falling blindly from one hour into the next—like water tossed from rock to rock, year after year down into uncertainty" (Hölderlin). As verse 2 has powerfully shown us it is not only my life and the meaning of my life that is at issue in essential loss. Each of us is and all of us alike stand under the same sentence of death. In seeking to break the spell of the nameless land and speak my own name, from the heart, I am not only seeking my self and a power of self-expression, I am seeking the human community in which heart might speak to heart and each name be remembered, treasured, and attended to. But this, in some ways, makes the task all the more difficult. Heidegger's vision asks of us the resolute courage that faces the ineluctable fact and that is ready, as he puts it, to run towards death. That is, in its way, admirable and even heroic—and perhaps, in his choice of words, Heidegger was only too conscious of the millions of his contemporaries who literally ran towards their deaths in the battlefields of Europe, each, in the end, in terrible isolation. But what Muir points to is a deepening of what, in relation to verse 1, we spoke of as heartbreak. Now, however, the trauma runs even deeper. Here we come to a point of infinite grief, in which we mourn not only the particular individuals we have loved and lost—though we do mourn them especially and in the first instance—but of all those "nameless" dead whose lives were the condition of our lives, without whom we would not and could not have been and, forgetful of whom, we too sink into namelessness, unable to progress across the "boundless plain" of eternally recurrent time.

In *Fear and Trembling* Kierkegaard conjures a vision of what life would be like

> if one generation emerged after another like leaves in a forest, if one generation succeeded another like the singing of birds in the forest, if a generation passed through the world as a ship through the sea, as wind through the desert, a thoughtless and fruitless activity, and if an eternal oblivion was constantly and voraciously on the look-out for its prey and there was no power strong enough to recue it—how empty and inconsolable life would be.[4]

Such a vision reduces not only the individual but the totality of human life, generation after generation, to meaninglessness. This is no longer "history" but mere succession, as in Nietzsche's view of the world as entirely devoid of aim, unity, or purpose. For Kierkegaard this situation is redeemed by the heroic faith of Abraham (as, for Nietzsche, it would be redeemed by Zarathustra and the teaching of the Superman, and, for Heidegger, by the act of resolutely running towards death). But Muir suggests that, in the first instance, we need to take time simply to let ourselves grieve, to find our sorrow, to discover that we do indeed sorrow and that it is only in sorrow and by sorrowing that a blessing might come at all. For the implicit premise of sorrow is that we love those we mourn, and this discovery of love is co-original with discovering the heart's power to listen, to speak, and to break. Finding ourselves in the "mystical body" of humanity, the society of the living and the dead (as Berdyaev put it) is the precondition for finding ourselves and finding meaning in the whole. But, to repeat, the first step is, simply, to find the time to let ourselves become open to the infinity of loss in which we are already encompassed—but who would wish to do that? How could it "come naturally"? But, equally, is it an "art" that could be taught? Certainly we need to learn it, but it is something more and far more basic than any life-skill we might acquire through self-help or life-coaching classes.

As we ponder whether, in the end, "art" is the right word for what the poet is asking us to learn, we note also another striking word, "resurrect": "Time, teach us the art / That *resurrects* the heart." But if "art" seems almost to say too little at this point, "resurrect" might seem to be saying too much.

---

4. Kierkegaard, *Fear and Trembling*, 15 (adapted).

Of course, we may hear in it no more than a strong and even an exaggerated metaphor, exaggerated to the point of hyperbole. Perhaps, "resurrect" means no more than "revive" or reawaken from a state of somnolence or a return after an absence. Perhaps the art that resurrects the heart is simply the same art that breaks and heals the heart, only expressed more dramatically. For the heart that must be broken and healed is, in a certain sense, neither more nor less than the heart that each of us already has. If we don't "have" it in the strong sense of being aware of it and inhabiting it as the centre of our moral and creative and personal lives, it is nevertheless there already, implicitly, or "potentially." Our task is merely to realize this potential for having a heart and to do so by letting it break and so begin also to be healed and become a listening, speaking heart.

But resurrection seems to suggest something more than realizing a potential. When early Christians proclaimed the resurrection of the body, their pagan auditors laughed at them since, they thought, a body that was dead could not come to life again and why, they asked, would one want it to, once the immortal soul that had inhabited it and given it life had departed? But Christianity itself already knew and emphasized from the beginning that resurrection is and must be miraculous. If Christ had simply swooned on the cross and been mistaken for dead, only to revive after a few hours' rest, this would not be a resurrection. It would not be the basis for a whole new way of looking at ourselves and our world. There is a moment of radical discontinuity in the transition from death to resurrection that goes far beyond anything suggested by reviving, or reawakening, or realizing a potential. But, perhaps, as I have suggested, the poem is only invoking resurrection here in order to give force to what, after all, is no more than reviving a weary heart or realizing a heart that has thus far been in abeyance, a merely potential heart! After all, Christianity itself has been happy enough to associate its preaching of Christ's resurrection with the yearly renewal of nature and to see in spring flowers an image for resurrection itself, whilst in the novel *Resurrection*, Tolstoy used the motif of "resurrection" for what, in the event, was the purely moral resurrection or regeneration of a corrupt personality. Not every occurrence of the word "resurrection" need immediately require assent to all that Christian doctrine has meant by the word. But is this really reducible to a matter of forceful expression?

Here too, as in the case of "the Word," it may be fruitful to allow for a certain indeterminacy or to permit a certain convergence between the purely human meaning of the word and its strong "theological" sense. Let us be open to the possibility that something far more world-changing is happening here than the normal realization of a natural potential, like the emergence of sexuality in adolescence. The latter will happen whether we like it or not and whether it occurs as an easy passage to adulthood or as a time of deep trauma that the unfortunate individual will never fully resolve! But what is being talked about here is certainly not something that will happen automatically or without our consent. If it is to happen at all we must make it happen, we must take the step of opening our hearts and letting the tears flow. Precisely because this is the moment in which the self breaks free from its determination as a purely natural self, subject to the law of generation and passing-away (like the leaves of the forest, as Kierkegaard put it), we experience it as the advent of a different kind of being, perhaps what Paul Tillich once called "the new being." Even if we are not yet talking about a literally dead body coming back to life, we can see how something like a passage from death to life might well provide an image for the coming of such a new being.

We seem to be moving towards a decisively Christian interpretation of what Muir is saying, and Christian tradition would be behind him in seeing the regeneration of the individual as, in some way, dependent on the resurrection of Christ, which is itself a pledge of a more general resurrection still to come. But, again, the fact that he speaks of learning resurrection as an "art" might seem to deflect the Christian reading. For what Christianity promises is a miracle, and miracles cannot be taught or made the subject of an "art." Yet we might remind ourselves that Muir has chosen this word in a verse that also speaks of death and of the relation of the present self to the great company of the departed. We have seen something of what the sense of our solidarity with the dead meant to Muir, and we do him the credit of having chosen his words with care. What we will learn when we learn this art will be something that gives us a possibility of living with a full, clear, and fully accepting understanding of our manifold relations to the dead and, with them, to our own death. Since it is death that is at issue, maybe we should not immediately foreclose on the possibility that resurrection is the resolution of all that is put in question by death.

Verse Three

I

Tongue, you can only say
Syllables, joy and pain,
Till time, having its way,
Makes the word live again.

The Heart Learning to Speak

If verse 2 began by addressing the heart and thereby moving from the third person commentary of verse 1 to the more intimate and personal mode of second person discourse, verse 3 starts with a further shift. It is no longer the heart that is being addressed but the tongue. More specifically, it is a tongue that has become able to speak of joy and pain but which, as of now, has not yet learned to work these "syllables" into coherent speech. May we, then, assume that this is the tongue of a heart that is no longer silent and no longer dumb but is beginning to speak? That it does so imperfectly, stutteringly perhaps, and maybe even incoherently is not to say that it is not speaking or that it says nothing. It has allowed itself to break and to feel pain, even if it has not yet felt all the pain of its essential loss or opened up to the all-encompassing grief of its relation to the dead. And, in the measure that it has learned pain and learned to utter the syllables that express its pain, it has also begun to learn healing and to have the intimations of joy that, in its own words, it is beginning to express as gratitude and love (or so we might guess). The closing lines of both verses 1 and 2 spoke of an art that had to be learned, and no art moves from the preliminary instruction to entire mastery in a single lesson or a single step. Like the infant human learning language, the heart that we now see learning the language of its new being is still only learning, still only a beginner, still not able to say all that it might want to say or will one day be able to say.

However, although these comments accord with what common sense might suppose, they suggest another angle from which the previous verse's invocation of "resurrection" might seem exaggerated. Isn't it precisely the point of a resurrection that it is a transition from one state (death) to another (life) "in the twinkling of an eye," in an instant? Isn't it irreducible to any causal chain or any process? Isn't the logic of resurrection the logic of a miracle? Doesn't it have to be essentially inexplicable? And if that is so, then how might one learn the meaning of resurrection gradually? Wouldn't that too—as Hume sarcastically remarked—have to be a miracle, an event in the life of the believer that simply couldn't be explained or fitted in to any biographical or intellectual narrative? Admittedly, the New Testament itself speaks of some of the newly converted as being like babes and needing to be fed with milk before they can go on to stronger spiritual meat, but does this negate the fundamental difference between a process of learning and conversion to faith in something essentially inexplicable, something that has to be believed in or hoped for but which can never be the subject of an art?

We shall return to this question shortly when we come to the last two lines where, as we shall see, the poet breaks the pattern of the previous two verses and asks for something that is not an art and asks not as one might ask a teacher for teaching but as one might ask a god for a blessing—asks, that is, in the manner of prayer.

For now, however, we shall continue to consider the heart that is still taking its first steps in learning to speak and reflect further on what might be involved in its becoming capable of progressing from these inarticulate syllables of joy and pain to being able to speak its word in the fullest sense. In doing so, it may be recalled that we have previously encountered a reference to "syllables," when, in "The Labyrinth," Muir depicts a world at peace with itself under the benign rule of a pantheon of deities. In describing this world, Muir speaks of the dialogue that the presiding gods hold amongst themselves as "easy utterance of harmonious words, / Spontaneous syllables bodying forth a world." The difference between the two cases is, of course, striking. In the one we are now considering the isolated syllables of joy and pain are indicative of the *in*ability of the newly speaking heart to express itself in coherent words, phrases, and sentences. In the case of the gods, however, the syllables they speak spontaneously and effortlessly "body forth" a world. Not only do they do this but, as we have seen, the world they body forth is a world in which all is well, all is as it should be, and mortals are at peace with one another, with the earth, and with their gods. Muir, we further recall, spoke of that as the "real world" and yet I also argued that it is nevertheless not the world we know or, for now, inhabit or even could inhabit.

We have several times noted how Muir depicts our common human life as bounded by time in such a way that we are always journeying and never arriving, in perpetual motion between an irretrievable starting-point and an "end" that cannot be anticipated. Yet there is something in this time-experience that distinguishes it from Nietzsche's eternal recurrence or Heidegger's being-towards-death. We have been separated from our origins and we never, in life, arrive at our end. Yet, even "we . . . here," in this "difficult land," have "one foot in Eden still": that is, we have a memory, a trace, a sense, no matter how minimal—even if it is perhaps only a memory of what has long been forgotten—of an ordered and harmonious world. And, looking forward, the evening light sometimes vouchsafes us a glimpse of the golden harvester assigned to gather all things in at the end of time. In this memory and in this hope we are sustained in our search in time for what, in "The Journey back" Muir calls "a man who has done good / His long lifelong and is / Image of man from whom all have diverged." And, even while we are still underway, we have such revelations as the golden age revealed to the poet as he struggles to find a way out of the labyrinth or a transfiguration, giving back, for an hour, "the clear unfallen world." And even though "the world / Rolled back into its place, and we are here, / And all that radiant kingdom lies forlorn" it has left behind the hope that "he will come again"—"he" being the one whose word made all things pure. Those who are fed by such visions will likely have the conviction that they are of "the real world" ("The Labyrinth") or of a world that "made this unreal" ("The Transfiguration"). Yet there is no definitive answer to the question "Was it a vision? / Or did we see that day the unseeable / One glory of the everlasting world / Perpetually at work, though never seen / Since Eden locked the gate that's everywhere / And nowhere?" ("The Transfiguration").

Our situation, then, is a strangely double one. We have "one foot in Eden" but are unable to extricate ourselves from "these fields that we have planted / So long with crops of love and hate." So deeply are our identities tied up with this ambiguity that we might even cease to know ourselves if we were suddenly to find ourselves transposed into a golden age or a transfigured world. The fact that in such a world as this our hearts cannot but be exposed to heartbreak is, we have seen, integral to their becoming capable of speech and capable of attending to the need of other hearts. In this situation we might discern what John Hick called a *"felix culpa"* theme in Muir's vision—that the fall that separates us for ever from the original harmony is in a mysterious way a "happy fault" that gives us something Eden alone could never have bestowed. Indeed "One Foot in Eden" says just this: that for those doomed to the world's "winter way" "famished field and blackened tree / Bear flowers in Eden never known. / Blossoms of grief and charity / Bloom in these darkened fields alone. / What had Eden ever to say / Of hope and faith and pity and love . . . Strange blessings never in Paradise / Fall from these beclouded skies."

"This life is our one chance of learning love"—the words are Browning's, but Muir would certainly have endorsed them. The golden age presided over by the eternal dialogue of the gods is a world of beauty, harmony, and peace, but it is not a world that has learned all there is to be learned of love, since this can only be learned through the happy fault of sharing fallen humanity's "winter way." If this is indeed what we learn, then time is no longer simply the destroyer but, as Pindar already knew, "the sole judge of Truth that shall abide" (Olympian 10.55). Nevertheless, in several of Muir's poems the negativity of time still has the upper hand. Love is tested by time and, in that sense, time can prove whether love is really love, but the question is really whether love is strong enough to resist or defy time. Thus, in "Love in Time's Despite" the poet affirms that "we who love and love again can dare / To keep in his despite our summer still, / Which flowered, but shall not wither, at his will." Time, as the title and first verse of that poem indicates is love's rival rather than love's friend. Even so, there are also hints of a more complex view. In "Love's Remorse," the poem immediately preceding "Love in Time's Despite," Muir writes of "the old saw still by the heart retold" that "Love is exempt from time." "And that is true," he adds, although immediately qualifying this with the further comment that it is "only the truth" that is "always new," whilst "we, the loved and the lover, we grow old." Here, then, is a complex interplay of time as effecting the irreversible and inevitable decay and annihilation of our human powers and as nevertheless also revealing the truth of love and, in that sense—perhaps!—bringing love to its highest fruition. Time—and this is certainly no new thought—is essentially ambiguous, a Janus-faced phenomenon that reveals a basic choice at the heart of human existence.

Let us turn once more to the philosophers, this time again to Berdyaev. We have already seen how Berdyaev's account of creative memory offers a way of imagining the trans-historical resurrection life in which we are now united with the dead and his conception of this life also involves him in postulating two very different sorts of time and, therewith, two very different sorts of history. Conscious both of Heidegger's attempt to return philosophy to the question of Being and of Neo-Thomism's revival of an older tradition of thinking of God as Being Itself, Berdyaev rejects both in favor of a "philosophy which recognizes the supremacy of freedom over being."[1] "Freedom," he says, "is without foundation; it is not determined by being nor born of it. There is no compact, uninterrupted being. There are breaks, fractions, abysses, paradoxes; there are transcensions. There exist, therefore, only freedom and personality."[2] Affirming in his own way Muir's insistence on the primacy of the personal, Berdyaev adds that "Personality is outside of all being. It stands in opposition to being . . . its principle is dissimilarity."[3] This is because each personal existence is "something new" in nature that never has been before and never will be again. "Personality is the exception, not the rule. The secret of the existence of personality lies in its absolute irreplaceability, its happening but once, its uniqueness, its incomparableness."[4] In other words, neither thinking of ourselves as being-towards-death nor thinking of ourselves as determined by a God who foreordained what we were to be before the foundations of the world were laid can ever adequately account for that unique irreplaceable event in the life of the world that each of us is; that you are, that I am.

Of course, it is always possible to explain a person's behavior on the plane of our common experience of history. There is nothing we can say or do that is not reducible to an individual instance of a general truth of some kind or other, biological, sociological, or historical. We can apply the laws of physics or biology to human beings in one or other aspect of their lives and explain each individual as merely an individual instance of a universal law. The same is true of history and the laws of history. We are subject to time and cannot escape the inescapable processes of time and its constant

1. Berdyaev, *Slavery and Freedom*, 75–76.

2. Ibid., 76.

3. Ibid., 80.

4. Ibid., 23; cf. Berdyaev, *Solitude and Society*, 68.

erosion of our physical and mental powers. But, for Berdyaev, there is also another time, and the "time" in which the creative novelty of each singular personal life exists is not the "horizontal" or "objectified" time running from past to present to future, a sequence of events crying out for and always susceptible to explanation. Instead, it is what Berdyaev at one time calls "super-history" and at another "existential time"; time that "happens in the vertical and not the horizontal."[5] The true time of existence, he suggests, is apocalyptic time, for "time is not the image of eternity . . . time is eternity that has collapsed in ruins"[6]—a vision that accords well with how "One Foot in Eden" evokes time as "tak[ing] the foliage and the fruit / And burn[ing] the archetypal leaf / To shapes of terror and of grief / Scattered along the winter way." Only in the prism of eschatological existence can contemporary existence become meaningful and fulfilled. But this has nothing to do with the kind of eschatological expectation involved when people scour the book of Revelation for the date of the second coming. Apocalyptic time does not lie on the surface of historical time to be discerned by means of signs and portents and still less read off from supposed laws of historical development. It is "in" time in the way that personality itself is "in" time, as a secret, as unique, as free, and as the possibility of "a new thing."

Does this, then, point to the kind of time that might be in play when time reveals the heart's truth and, in doing so, "makes the word live again"? If this is so, then the manner in which that word will come to expression will be very different from the deep harmonies of the eternal dialogue of the gods. It will, to borrow Berdyaev's terms, be a word marked by "fractions, abysses, paradoxes," bearing the scars of suffering and of contrition for time ill-used. It will be a word spoken with all the passion of a human heart living in time and exposed to all the negativity of time, a heart heavy with need and longing but also a heart now finding the freedom to speak. And learning to speak, we recall, is never something that an individual does by him- or herself alone. We learn to speak only when there is one to listen; only when there is someone to attend to our need; only when there is a witness to our life whom we can trust with our first, faltering attempts to speak our truth.

This reciprocity is beautifully, concisely, and paradigmatically articulated in the first of Muir's poems on "The Annunciation," when he speaks

5. Berdyaev, *The Beginning and the End*, 163.

6. Ibid., 207.

of "the liberty / Where each asks from each / What each most wants to give / And each awakes in each / What else would never be." That time provides not only the occasion for such speech but is in a deeper sense integral to it is perhaps implicit in the last two lines just quoted, since what each awakes in each is precisely something that can only come about when the word of love is freely spoken. What is said is a new thing. It is not so much a matter of realizing or actualizing a potential that each of the speakers already has but of their words of love releasing an entirely new possibility into the world: it is a resurrection of the heart and not simply a recovery or revival of a merely weakened or somnolent heart. In verse 3 of "The Annunciation" Muir underlines the ineluctably temporal nature of this word, by warning himself against bestowing "some more than mortal grace" on the beloved and therefore deifying her, "forgetting love was born / Here in time and place." As in "One Foot in Eden," a timeless world, no matter how perfect, would have nothing to say "of hope and faith and pity and love." The word that speaks forth such things must be a word spoken in time: yet it is also, somehow, from beyond time or from another time, from a time to come, even, the time when the golden harvester gathers all things in. But how might we (in time, the time that now is) hear such a word, how might we prepare ourselves to hear it?

The Moment of Vision

One answer as to how we might prepare ourselves to hear the saving word is hinted at in the comment that it is time "having its way" that "makes the word live again." This suggests that the best strategy for us is, simply, to let time have its way and, in particular, have its way with us. It is a curious phrase, such as we might use of a headstrong child or a seducer (and perhaps time is not entirely unlike both of these). In any case, it seems to suggest that the task is not so much maintaining love "in time's despite" as letting ourselves go along with whatever time is doing to us and with us.

In our first reflections on time, it was time's way of having its way with us that was precisely the problem, since it seemed that the one sure outcome of life in time was that we would be used up, emptied out, and cast into oblivion, like grass thrown into the oven, as Psalm 103 puts it. But we have now seen from several angles how "time" is no merely negative power but also contributes creatively to the birth of the word or even "the Word." So, here, the statement that it is time that, "having its way," will make "the word live again" points to a creative role for time, as if it is *time itself* that will make us capable of speaking and hearing living words. Time is not just running on from infinity to infinity or recurring eternally but leads us towards and provides the conditions for a decisive moment of liberation from all that—in time—oppresses us.

There can be no question for Muir of any laws of history surely bringing about a future redemption, as if history was a kind of machine programmed to bring about a determinate outcome. Precisely because the "outcome" is the speaking of the liberating word that calls for freely given attention on the part of speaker and listener time will not do all the work for us. But the realization that what we are seeking and what alone will satisfy us is a living and not an abstract word is something we can learn from time; that is, from the fact that our lives are lived in time. Without time we would be without memories and hopes and it is through the interplay of these with our present responsibilities that we are able to become genuinely personal beings, bearers of a coherent identity and of a definite complex of moral and other core human values. Time as we experience it does not simply flow from past to future in a uniform or monotonous way, but the ebbs, flows, and whirlpools of time pattern our lives, bringing us to times of decision but also giving us frequent pause for thought. Although it repeatedly throws us into situations for which we are not yet ready, time also heals and without it recovery from physical or mental trauma would be impossible. Letting time have its way, then, is to surrender to the inescapable reality that, in the end, time will certainly carry us away "and our place shall know us no more." That we are creatures of time means, as we have seen, that we are marked by essential loss, in every cell of our body and in every thought of our mind. Yet it is no less true that the destroyer is also, in a sense, the creator, and it is time that makes it possible for life to be life in the fullest sense of the word and not just a static and featureless state of being—life, endlessly bubbling up and pouring itself out in ceaseless sensation and vibrancy: *Life, Life*, as the title of a recent book by Don Cupitt has it!

But to experience time in this way, as abundance of life, is no longer to experience it simply as a "teacher" in any conventional sense. Time is not a power standing over against us and instructing us in something of which we would otherwise have no experience or knowledge. Time is within us, it permeates and even *is* our very being: that we are and *are* at all and are *as we are* is possible only because we are time's own children. Whether or not there is anything more to our lives than what they are "in time" it is impossible entirely to separate our lives out from what we might call the time of our lives. Therefore, it is not enough to be taught by time if we really want to learn all that time has to teach us: we have to let time have its way with us, surrendering ourselves to its embrace, and giving it time to do all that is within its power to do with us.

This way of putting it nevertheless suggests that, however little we may be able to contribute to this process, we still have to do something. After all, even if we cannot ultimately ward off the nothingness to which time will eventually bring us, we often seem to be busy with strategies for putting off the impending day or for heroically but hopelessly resisting time's implacable march. Something is asked of us, something must happen to us or with us if we are to let time have its way. We have to come to be in relation to time in another way from how we are when time is nothing but the harbinger of essential loss. An act of surrender too is a decision—so what and how must we decide to be in relation to the time that, even now and ever since we are born, is and has been the time of our lives? To address this question, we turn once more to the existential thinkers, to Kierkegaard, Heidegger, and the theological existentialist, Paul Tillich.

We have in the last section seen several examples of poems recording moments of intense illumination. Some have been of a golden age or of a timeless divine world, whilst others, most notably "The Transfiguration," have pointed to an experience in which the here-and-now, the soiled and even dangerous world in which we are now living is seen in another light and experienced as reconciled with itself. We interpreted what is happening in such transfiguring moments with the help of Berdyaev's notion of the apocalyptic or vertical time that breaks in on the "horizontal" time of worldly history and redeems it from self-ruination. But is such an "other" time essentially alien to what we experience in the ordinary horizontal time, even if, with Berdyaev, we might speak of it as a "secret" time within time?

Berdyaev's dualism and the violent associations of a term such as "apocalyptic" suggest or at least emphasize the element of radical *dis*continuity. But is our worldly experience of time solely of time that is "ruined" or can our time too, the time of our common human life, also serve the coming of this other, redemptive time? Does our ordinary time itself contain hints as to the secret that is to redeem it? In what follows I shall explore the possibility that this is indeed the case by reference to the existentialist idea of "the moment" or "moment of vision." In doing so, we shall see how the coming of apocalyptic time revealed in such visions as that of "The

Transfiguration" does not merely disrupt but also, in some sense, fulfills what is already at work in time. To some extent the main point here has already been anticipated in the preceding section: what we are seeking now is merely to clarify further the nature of that point at which our two times intersect or at which the one supervenes upon or is infused into the other.

The need for a "moment of vision" is first articulated by Kierkegaard, who sees it as necessary if time is not to be simply an infinite vanishing and our experience of time is not to be solely that of the endless cascade into nothingness that Hölderlin's *Hyperion* so powerfully evoked. In normal parlance, a "moment" is a part of the problem of time rather than its solution. As Augustine already observed, if the past is no more and the future is not yet, the moment has already flashed past in the instant I think of it: "now" is always already gone! This, however, is not what Kierkegaard means by "the moment" or (which is a more literal translation of the Danish Øjeblikket) "the moment of vision." A moment like this is not one more in an infinite stream of ephemeral moments but a moment in which I become conscious of myself and my world in a decisive fashion. In this moment the world becomes present to me and I see it for what and how it is. But, for Kierkegaard, this is only possible because whilst each "now" is consumed in the infinite succession of horizontal time, the eternal is also present in it or to it. That this is so means that whilst the "now" is the most fleeting of any of the three dimensions of time, it is only in the now and in relation to what is truly present in the now that we can apprehend the eternal and therefore also apprehend time as having a significance that is more than merely "temporal." As Kierkegaard put it in a discourse on the theme of "Joy:

> What is joy or what is being joyful? In truth, it is to be present to oneself. But to be present to oneself in truth, that is this "today": it is this—to *be* today, in truth to *be today*. And to the same degree that it is true that you *are* today, and in the same degree that you are entirely present to yourself in being today, in that same degree will misfortune's "next day" not exist for you. Joy is the present time, where the entire stress lies on *the present time*. That is why God is blessed, for in all eternity He says, "Today"—He who is eternally and infinitely present to Himself in being today. And that is why the lily and the bird are joy, because silently and obediently they are entirely present to themselves in being today.[7]

7. Kierkegaard, *Kierkegaard's Spiritual Writings*, 215.

In more theoretical language, Kierkegaard writes in *The Concept of Anxiety* that "the moment is that ambiguity in which time and eternity touch each other, and with this the concept of *temporality* is posited, whereby time constantly intersects eternity and eternity constantly pervades time." Yet if, as we have seen, the present has a certain privilege in relation to the experience of the eternal as present in and to time, Kierkegaard also says that "the future in a certain sense signifies more than the present and the past . . . [and] . . . the eternal first signifies the future or . . . the future is the incognito in which the eternal, even though it is incommensurable with time, nevertheless preserves its association with time."[8] And, as he goes on to note, this association is also reflected in the way in which many people spontaneously talk about the "future life" and "eternal life" as essentially synonymous.

Is Kierkegaard, then, inconsistent with regard to the relationship between present, future, and the eternal? I think not, and I think not because, on Kierkegaard's view of the human subject, we are as we are in the here and now by virtue of our orientation towards the future. It may be true that a child asks "Where did I come from" before it asks "What am I going to do be when I grow up," but, in a Kierkegaardian perspective, the first question is always in a sense a reflex of the second: as the child ponders the possibilities into which it has been "thrown" (to use Heidegger's image) the question as to its origin arises as a necessary preliminary to deciding what it is capable of, or what kind of being it is. We are, or, better, we become who we are through our choices, through how we relate to our possibilities, and this means always in relation to some possible future—whether we are talking about "When I grow up I want to be a spaceman" or simply "I'd like porridge for breakfast." But such a relation to the future, if it is not to be mere fantasy, must also be grounded in an understanding of myself as present, here and now.

Present and future are thus deeply intertwined. My presence to myself as a person capable of making a decision and relating myself to the future is revealed only in the mirror of that future itself. My question as to who I am is always a question as to who I am to be and yet it is also a question in which my future calls to me in my present. As Kierkegaard puts it in another discourse, in the moment in which a person first asks what the world means to them and what they mean to the world, they become "older than the moment." Such a person is no longer a transient link in

8. Kierkegaard, *The Concept of Anxiety*, 89.

an infinitely vanishing chain but is in the process of acquiring coherence and endurance. My present becomes significant because it is revealed as an aspect of a life in which there are choices still to be made. It is at this point, Kierkegaard also suggests, that the past comes into play, since if my choices vis-à-vis the future are not to be merely arbitrary or fanciful I must also take account of my past and how the person I am now has grown out of a particular life-story and is limited by a particular set of life-circumstances. In thus acquiring what he at one time calls an "inner history" my life begins to be redeemed from mere transience and I begin to live as "Spirit." "Thus understood," he says, "the moment is not properly an atom of time but an atom of eternity."[9] As such it is also (he says) what the New Testament refers to as the fullness of time, which he also calls "the pivotal concept in Christianity, that which made all things new."[10]

This is a crucial connection, since it implies that "the moment of vision," the decisive moment in which time is transformed by being brought into connection with the eternal, is not lacking in history. In the New Testament itself, the expression occurs when Jesus is described coming into Galilee and preaching "The time is fulfilled [or, in older translations 'at hand']: the Kingdom of God is upon you" (Mark 1:15). The idea is also taken up in the teaching that Christ's own coming occurred "in the fullness of time" (Col 1:10). In both cases it suggests that God's purposes cannot be fulfilled at just any time, but there is a *right* time, a time that is prepared for in a particular sequence of historical events. Whereas in the Platonic scheme truth is equally near and equally far from human beings at all times, the biblical narrative suggests that God's relation to human beings is, as it were "timed." Particular moments of time have particular significance and provide the unique occasion for a specific encounter with or response to the divine purpose—and it is in this sense also that Jesus can speak of Jerusalem not recognizing the "hour of its visitation" (Luke 19:44). Time qualified in this way is no longer simply *chronos*, time measured by the movement of celestial bodies or the ticking of a clock, but what the New Testament calls *kairos*: time for decision.[11]

---

9. Ibid., 88.

10. Ibid., 90.

11. Although James Barr has demonstrated that the distinction between *chronos* and *kairos* is not as sharp in the New Testament itself as it has been presented here, it is a distinction that has entered into the vocabulary of modern theology and it is in this modern sense that I am using it. See James Barr, *Biblical Words for Time*.

Of course, both Kierkegaard and the New Testament presuppose that history is governed by divine Providence and that time does not simply come to the moment of fulfillment of its own accord but is rather guided to that point by God's ceaselessly active and infinitely wise ordering of events. Yet even God, we might say, cannot act without or in contravention to the orders and rhythms of time: in order to come to be in time, God has to be "on time," to "come in," in a musical sense, at just the right time.

Paul Tillich drew out this idea in suggesting that not only is there a once-for-all time, uniquely realized in the time when the Word became flesh in the man Jesus, but that the lives of nations and individuals have a similar movement towards moments of fulfillment, moments that confront those who experience them with, literally, momentous decisions as to their common or individual future life in time. In a play on the New Testament idea of *kairos*, Tillich spoke of our general time-experience as being marked by such lesser *kairoi*, each of which had something of the character of the great once-for-all *kairos*: and just as this latter gives meaning to time as such, so the former give meaning to individual or communal experiences of time—as in those special times when lovers fall in love or renew their vows after betrayal or when a nation must make a great historical decision. He connected this also with the idea of fate: whereas the Platonic ideas are above time in such a way as not to be altered in any way by the alterations of time, an idea or a truth that is accessible only at "the right time," in the moment of *kairos*, has a fateful quality such that whether I come to know it or not is dependent on my seizing the time and responding to the moment of destiny that gives me the possibility of relating to it in a decisive way. "The moment of vision," then, since it has this character of *kairos* or fulfilled time, is not a brute interruption of horizontal time but is always a moment to which horizontal time is leading us and in which horizontal time finds its fulfillment—so that perhaps we should say that horizontal time is not really horizontal at all but curved, curving up towards or away from those supreme *kairos* moments that are to be seized in acts of free acceptance and giving. To know the moment of vision, then, I must, in a sense, let time itself have its way with me. These moments cannot happen at just any time and only time can tell us when the right time has come.[12]

But can time bring us to such a moment of vision without presupposing a providential and even Christ-centered view of history? For both

---

12. See Tillich, *Systematic Theology* III, 393–96. However, it is an idea he also discusses at many other places in his work.

Kierkegaard and Tillich, this is, in a sense, a given. So, for Tillich, the possibility of there being particular *kairoi* in my life in and through which I define my identity in a unique and distinctive way is a reflection of the once-for-all *kairos* of the coming of God in time. As he puts it in a sermon on "The Right Time" "When God himself appears in a moment of time, when he himself subjects himself to the flux of time, the flux of time is conquered. And if this happens in one moment of time, then all moments of time receive another significance."[13]

Heidegger offers an account of the moment of vision in which such a providential background is lacking. Much of his description of this moment can be correlated very closely with Kierkegaard's account. Quite apart from the fact that he uses what he acknowledged was Kierkegaard's own distinctive terminology, the relation of anticipated future possibility, present, and past is essentially identical with that found in *The Concept of Anxiety*. However, there is nothing corresponding to "the eternal" in Heidegger's account and the whole weight of what happens in the moment is borne not by the presence of the eternal but by the resolute self-choice of the existing subject. It is, he says, "the resolute rapture with which Dasein is carried away to whatever possibilities and circumstances are encountered in the Situation [i.e. the present] as possible objects of concern, but a rapture which is held in resoluteness" (BT, 338 / 387). The ground on which this occurs is and, for Heidegger, only can be the "groundless" ground of Dasein's being "thrown" towards its own annihilation in death. Thus there can be no *kairos* since all time is equally evacuated of intrinsic meaning by the all-encompassing nothingness. As a result, and, perhaps strangely for a philosophy in which time is so central, time itself contributes nothing to bringing us closer to the possibility of such a moment of fulfillment. At least in the perspective of *Being and Time*, it is only by sober reflection that we can be brought to see the necessity of choosing ourselves in a moment of vision that is also a moment of decision with regard to how we are to relate ourselves to the beings that we are. What we see in Heidegger's moment of vision is how we are thrown towards nothingness and, without any expectation of being consoled for the "essential loss" that encompasses our lives on every side and in every way, choosing ourselves as just such a "thrown" nothingness. We, it seems, are nothing but time and time is nothing but ceaseless annihilation. But being able to recognize this is precisely the hinge on which it is possible—if we have the courage for it—to attain an "authentic" relation

13. Tillich, *The Boundaries of our Being*, 276

to our own Being; that is, to relate to ourselves as we in truth are: nothing. For Heidegger, then, letting time have its way would be a counsel of despair even though time is the ultimate horizon of our entire existence. Choosing ourselves as temporal is an attempt to transcend time, to do more with time than time itself would let us do, left to itself. And, as we have previously seen, it is also a choice in which there is no word, only the silence that calls to us from the nothingness into which our lives are even now vanishing.

Yet, in his later philosophy, and still without invoking the Christian God, Heidegger too comes to speak of a "history of Being" in which time, although still the horizon within which all our experiences and understandings of Being are located, is no longer ultimate, but itself "given." As he puts it in a late lecture "On Time and Being," *"es gibt Zeit"* ("it gives time" or "time is given").[14] "Given" by what or by whom? In his lectures on Hölderlin from the 1930s it is in fact the poet, whose "word" grounds historicity and thereby "gives" time to his people. Perhaps, later—though Heidegger is never more elusive and allusive than here—it is the "Being" that is beyond all beings and beyond what metaphysics has thought of as Being (being that he sometimes writes under erasure) that gives time. Such a Being would no longer be a first principle or a supreme Being, but something that was essentially "different" from being, yet, nevertheless, giving itself to us as Being and as time. But when time and Being are understood as "given" by something that is neither time nor Being it once more becomes possible to think of time itself as having a history that recedes from or approaches a moment when vision is possible, a *kairos* or time of fulfillment. And once we allow for such a history then we must wait on time and time's own movement towards fulfillment to see, to hear, or otherwise to attend to what it is that gives us time and to how time, our time, can find fulfillment. And perhaps, if Heidegger's lectures on Hölderlin carry any weight, that will also mean attending to, listening out for, and being ready to listen to *a word*.

All this is by way of comment on Muir's suggestion that finding the word we need to free us for a love that embraces the dead and the living might involve letting time have its way. But if we do let time have its way and time itself brings us to the moment of vision and transformation that we are seeking, if, in and through time, we become capable of speaking and hearing that word, is that word itself a word that, so to speak, rises from and falls back into the flux of time? Or is it, as Kierkegaard and Tillich might suggest, a word that speaks to us of the eternal and even a word spoken to

14. Heidegger, *Zur Sache des Denkens*, 5ff.

us *by* the Eternal? But if that were to be so, how might we experience the meeting of time and eternity in the moment of vision itself? Would such a "rapture" (to use Heidegger's term) be a kind of mystical elevation beyond language? But if it were, how would it enable us to speak the needed word of love? Might such a moment itself have the character of a word? And, if so, what kind of word?

II

Time, merciful lord,
Grant us to learn your word.

The Prayer

The two lines that close the poem echo the closing couplets of the preceding
verses. Each couplet begins with the word "time." On this occasion, however, the poet is not asking for time to instruct him in any art. Rather, he
speaks in the manner of prayer, "Time, merciful lord . . ." But is it possible
for those who have internalized the crisis of modernity to pray or to do so
honestly? And what might such prayer mean? Such questions had already
engaged Muir in *We Moderns*, where, in discussing "the tragic view" of life
consequent upon Nietzsche, he wrote the following: "Prayer was in former
times the channel whereby a profound current of spiritual life flowed into
the lives of men and enriched them. This source of wealth has now almost
ceased, and Man has become less spiritual, more impoverished. We must
seek a new form of prayer. Better not to live at all than live without reverence and gratitude! Let our sacramental attitude to Life be our form of
prayer."[15]

Like much in these early essays, this comment is suggestive rather
than definitive, but what does seem clear is that if there is to be prayer at
all, and if we are to become capable of reverence and gratitude it must be a
"new form of prayer." I take it that this is to be understood as critical of the
kind of simple petitionary prayer that asks God for specific benefits such
as good weather, good health, or success in our worldly undertakings. If,
now, in this late poem, Muir concludes with a prayer, does this mean that
he has, in the end, reverted to what in *We Moderns* he thought had been left
behind, or is this in fact the kind of prayer that might count as "a new form
of prayer"? What does the prayer itself say?

What is immediately striking in these closing words is that time is no
longer figured as a mere teacher (as in the previous verses) but as a "merciful lord." Whereas a teacher can, in the end, teach no more than the pupil is

---

15. Moore [Muir], *We Moderns*, 236.

able to receive and therefore cannot in every case ensure that the outcome of the learning process will be as desired—the teacher cannot guarantee that the learner will really learn—a lord is a figure imbued with sovereignty: a lord has power to grant the fulfillment of what is being asked and can bring it about that what is commanded is also done; in this case, that the word really will be learned. To address time in this way, then, is almost to address time as a god or, let us say, as "God," since God too is addressed by believers as both "merciful" and as "Lord."

This distinction between a teacher and a god will be familiar to readers of Kierkegaard's *Philosophical Fragments*, where he explores the limits of what a teacher can do by reference to Socrates and Socrates' own account of his pedagogical practice as a kind of midwifery, drawing out from the pupil what the pupil already knows. Kierkegaard labeled this "recollection," suggesting that the job of a teacher in such a case is simply to remind the pupil of what he already knows or to direct him to what he is, in fact, capable of. By way of contrast, if there was a truth that lay utterly beyond the capacity of the learner, then the teacher would not only have to guide him to it but also give him the condition for learning it when he found it. Such a teacher would have to bring about a transformation of the very identity—the being—of the learner and, Kierkegaard further argues, only a god would be capable of doing this. Such a God, as he points out, is no longer a teacher but a redeemer or savior.

But this provokes a further thought. Perhaps it is not time that is being addressed here at all. Perhaps it actually is God! Whereas in verse 1 the use of a capital "W" in Word led us to think of the divine Word of St John's Gospel—although we then had to concede that Muir might, nevertheless, simply be referring to a word such as two human beings can speak to each other—so here we might be being misled by the lower-case "l" to think that it is a merely creaturely lord, such as time, being addressed, when it is "The Lord," the Creator, who is, as such, also Lord and Creator of time. Thus, instead of asking the merciful lord called "Time" to grant us to learn his word (lower-case "w" this time!), these lines might be asking the merciful Lord who is God and Lord of all to grant us time that we might learn his Word—as in the old Anglican form of absolution that asks God for "time for amendment of life."

Do we have to choose between such interpretations? In discussing whether "the Word" was best considered as the divine Word or as a simple human word "from the heart," we drew attention to how Muir could only conceive of a divine Word as beneficial for human beings when it was a Word *made flesh*. And we also saw from Bultmann's commentary on the Prologue of St John's Gospel that the divine Word-made-flesh itself needed the testimony of human words—words of love spoken by one human being to another—if it was to become a word we were capable of hearing and a word to which we might respond. Here too: if we consider that learning the word is, in the end, only possible as the merciful gift of a Lord who speaks to us from beyond time we must nevertheless hear it as a word spoken *in* time and, more specifically, spoken to us in the very specific time of our lives; conversely, when the words we speak to one another in time become capable of asking each what each most wants to give and awakening in each what else would never be, then they are becoming words that point us beyond the ruined time manifest in the change, decay, and annihilation of mortal powers. A love that reveals its truth "in time's despite" is pointing to a kind of time that is different from the time that is exhausted in being-towards-death. It is not pointing us *beyond* time to an eternal, timeless divine world, but it is calling us to a *different* time or to a different *kind* of time. This is the time revealed in the "moment of vision," the *kairos*, which is also the paradoxical intersection of time and the eternal.

What, then, is being asked for in these last two lines? If they are addressed to time, they are asking that we might learn time's word, but if addressed to God, that we might be given time to learn the divine word. But what, exactly, is the difference? In each case, the word is precisely the word that a speaking heart will want to speak, a word of love, and if that is so then, in each case, we are not praying for liberation from the ruined time of historical existence (as if we might, somehow, shed our historical skins), but for a "strange blessing" uniquely proper to such time. It is praying for a moment of vision in which horizontal is intersected by vertical time; or it is praying for ruined time to be transfigured in the light of eschatological time; and, in every case, it is praying that we might learn to hear "the Word" (whether human or divine) in such a way that our human hearts might become able to speak both their grief and their charity. But is such a blessing possible, is it even conceivable within the experience of historical time? Berdyaev spoke of the advent of apocalyptic time as the occurrence of a new thing—but is such a thing too new for us to conceive or even imagine? Where might we find it that we might seek it?

In the light of everything we have considered about the power of time construed as being-towards-death and also in the light of the challenge posed by our present technological age to a heart that aches to speak but cannot find the words, it is perhaps no wonder if we start to think that the liberating word might, in the end, have to be spoken to us from beyond time or, at least, from beyond the time that holds sway in this present age. No matter how close time's way brings us to the moment of revelation, something more, it seems, is needed. In an age when the ancient fissure running through the human world has broken open and scattered the peoples of the world in a seemingly endless flight from war, poverty, and the break-up of nations and relationships, and when even our so-called communication technologies often serve only to isolate us all the more from one another, distracting us from what we really need to be saying to each other, where are we to find a word that might free the heart to speak its word? In an interview given in 1966 but only published ten years later, after his death, Heidegger spoke of how, in relation to the age of planetary technology "only a god can save us." Whatever Heidegger might have meant by that (and it has been much debated) it suggests that it is not a teacher we need but a *savior*, one who not only instructs us by pointing us back Socratically to what we are already capable of, but one who bestows a new possibility on us, a possibility of love we long for but cannot give ourselves. And perhaps—some remarks of Heidegger suggest this—it is the peculiar Socratic pedagogy of this age of technology that it is drawing our attention not to the truth that we already have *within* us but that the truth we need, the truth that would make our lives and being whole, is *beyond* us and beyond us in such a way that all we can do is to wait upon it.

But how might we—how do we—articulate our need for a possibility we cannot give ourselves, a possibility for which we can only wait? I have already suggested that these two lines have a form resembling that of prayer and prayer would seem to be precisely the mode of speech fitted to such an impossible possibility, the mode of speech natural to longing, seeking, yearning, desiring, and needing what we cannot give ourselves, whether that is something necessary for our biological survival or the love of another human being. Now there is no doubt that many practices of prayer sell human possibilities short. Kant famously remarked that we would be embarrassed to be caught praying since to pray for something indicates a refusal of the responsibility and autonomy proper to being human. But if that is what prayer does, it may be that it is only because the institutionalization of prayer in authoritarian ecclesiastical cultures has taught men and women to pray for what they can, in fact, achieve themselves. To the extent that such cultures are allowed to define what prayer is, then Kant has at least a relative right on his side. But what if, as many religious teachers insist, prayer really begins only at the limit of human possibilities, *really at the limit* of human possibilities? But, then, if we have really arrived at such a limit how can prayer find voice in language? For what could we find to say when all our accepted ways of being human had been exhausted as, at the outermost limit, they must be? How, then, in those situations that most call for prayer—when we most feel the need to pray—can we actually pray? What should we do? What should we say?

The question is not merely rhetorical but is asked in the light of believers' own testimony to the nature of prayer. Paul the apostle already speaks of "sighs and groans too deep for words," whilst mystical traditions, past and present, in East and West, give an emphatic place to silence as a crucial element in the practice of prayer. When the disciples asked Jesus "teach us to pray" this might be taken as a mere formula, an almost ritual request such as disciples of a religious teacher might be expected to ask. But if we take seriously what has been said in the last few lines, praying seems not to be so easy and might well be something we need to be instructed in—not from mere curiosity but in order that we might learn the one thing needful, the "thing" on which our whole life—our salvation—depends. If, then, we are to speak of what it might mean to think of ourselves and our situation as being redeemable only through the action of a god, we must learn the language of prayer—but does prayer have a language and, if so, how might we learn it?

In reflecting on verse 1, I associated Muir's reflections on the heart's need to speak with what I called "the lyric moment" in Romantic literary practice, a moment paradigmatically realized in the unchained melodies of the skylark and nightingale. Were we to find it, such a lyric moment might give relief to us weary citizens of an age of technology that is also an age of anxiety, misunderstandings, lies, and violence. Were we to find it! But, as Andersen's story of the Emperor and the Nightingale suggested, such a possibility, even if it still exists in our technological age, can only exist as a secret, at a tangent to all that preoccupies us in our busy, serious, commerce with reality. It is a song, but a song without words.

Kierkegaard already dismissed what he called the "poetic" cult of pure song as empty longing. In the real world, the lyric moment is a utopia, it is nowhere and nothing. But Kierkegaard does not simply dismiss the poet, instead he transposes the poet's song into prayer. Like the Romantic poets,

Kierkegaard too liked to go out into nature, to be alone with the birds and the flowers and, under the guidance of the Sermon on the Mount, he wrote many religious discourses on "The Lilies of the Field and the Birds of the Air." These provided him with an alternative experience of life to what he endured in the "human swarm" of an urban culture undergoing rapid modernization. Especially concise are the three discourses on this theme published as a small volume in 1849. Under the titles "Silence," "Obedience," and "Joy" the discourses expound the gospel injunction to consider the lilies and the birds. In these discourses he contrasts the different ways in which the poet and the gospel speak about nature. The poet goes no further than the desire to be like the lilies and the birds. Entranced by the joy he hears pouring forth from the bird, he too aches to sing such a song as might teach a similar joy to the world. But, in the end, all he has to say boils down to "If only . . ." His exalted moods and his penchant for secrecy are equally indicative of the fact that it is in the end mere fantasy.[16] The gospel, by way of contrast, proposes to our contemplation the lilies and birds, which, Kierkegaard says, offer genuine instruction in the possibility of self-transformation—if only we could learn to become (like them) silent, (like them) obedient, and (like them) joyful. But, as the discourses on silence and obedience especially emphasize, this is only possible if we learn not only to be silent but also to attend to what is being said to us in silence. He writes:

> And what happened then, if you did indeed pray with real inwardness? Something wonderful. For as you prayed more and more inwardly, you had less and less to say, and finally you became entirely silent. You became silent and, if it is possible that there is something even more opposed to speaking than silence, you became a listener. You had thought that praying was about speaking: you learned that praying is not merely keeping silent but is listening. That is how it is. Praying is not listening to oneself speak, but is about becoming silent and, in becoming silent, waiting, until the one who prays hears God.[17]

I shall shortly return to the point that what we are to attend to is—despite what Kierkegaard says here about silence—something *said*, but before

---

16. Would this also fit the case of one like Hölderlin who, in Heidegger's interpretation, knows himself to be bound to the barren time of need between the flight of the old gods and the advent of the new?

17. Kierkegaard, *Kierkegaard's Spiritual Writings*, 185.

doing so I want to make a couple of further comments concerning what we are to learn from the lilies and the birds. In the first instance, learning from them involves us in becoming attentive to who we ourselves are in this present moment and, as we have seen, this is what Kierkegaard regards as the secret and the reality of joy (to repeat): "What is joy or what is being joyful? In truth, it is to be present to oneself. . . . That is why God is blessed, for in all eternity He says, 'Today'—He who is eternally and infinitely present to Himself in being today. And that is why the lily and the bird are joy, because silently and obediently they are entirely present to themselves in being today."[18] But such presence to self is possible only on the basis of also silently and obediently attending to God—but where do we find God in order to attend to him? In these discourses, Kierkegaard's answer is that we find him by going out and "beholding" the lilies and the birds, by reminding ourselves of and imaginatively re-situating ourselves in the original God-relationship of creature to creator.

At this point, however, it might be objected that, although we, like the lilies and the birds, are creatures, we are a very different kind of creature, the human creature, and there are significant dissimilarities between us and them. As Kierkegaard himself points out, neither the lilies nor the birds *think* about God. They merely are what they are and it is precisely by being what and as they are (i.e., by being lilies and birds) that they fulfill God's purpose for them. In principle, at least, it is no different in the case of human beings. As Kierkegaard had argued in an earlier set of discourses on the same text, one thing we learn from the lilies and the birds is the glory of simply being human and being content with simply being human. But, obviously, human beings are not flowers or birds. Flowers and birds are as they are, but we are able to choose who we are—or, for that matter, to choose not to be who we are and to try to become something or someone else and to flee from ourselves in bad faith and inauthenticity. The self-relation inherent in our human way of being means that something more is required of us than is required of the lilies and the birds. This means, in the first instance, that we must want that "more," but to want it is already, in his view, to begin to pray—for what, in the end, is prayer but the articulation of what we really, most deeply, and most passionately want and cannot give ourselves?

We are, perhaps, beginning to pray. But to pray is not only to long for something, it is (or so I have just implied) also to articulate that longing and

18. Ibid., 215.

to do so in words. Moreover, in this particular case, in Muir's poem, what the one praying is asking for is neither more nor less than *to learn a word*! But what, then, of everything we have just been hearing about silence, the silence we are to learn from the lilies and the birds? This is not just a matter of what Kierkegaard says in these discourses nor, for that matter, in his other spiritual writings. For on this point at least (and as previously noted) Kierkegaard is in continuity with a broad stream of Christian spiritual writing. That prayer is, in the end, an initiation into silence, into an encounter with God that is beyond words, would seem to be integral to what we might call the perennial philosophy of prayer, within and beyond Christianity. By insisting on and even praying for "a word" are we not tying prayer down to an overly anthropomorphic model of God, who "listens to" and "answers" prayers? Isn't real prayer, the prayer of saints and mystics, something rather different from presenting a list of petitions? Isn't it simply learning to be with God, in silent contemplation—what some French spiritual directors called "the prayer of simple regard"? Isn't it about *being* rather than speaking? And, if that is so, merely to say "Thou" is already—dangerously—to bring God down to a human level and to disturb the silence in which the soul is not only alone with but one with God.

And yet this deeply engrained idea that there may be two essentially different kinds of prayer corresponding to two essentially different conceptions of God (and, consequently, of the human God-relationship) may reflect a misunderstanding, both of silence and of God. In his book *The Ark of Speech*, Jean-Louis Chrétien has written a chapter on "The Hospitality of Silence" in which he proposes that only "a creature of speech" (such as the human being) can fall silent: "[S]ilence cannot manifest itself . . . except to someone who is able to speak." And, he continues, speech itself "comes from the silence that always precedes it . . . it accompanies silence, for while it is being uttered, it needs the noises all around and the lips of the other whom it is addressing to be silent: it ends towards silence, which alone can ratify that it has in truth said something and which allows the other to speak . . ."[19] In this regard, he goes on to make a strong distinction between the kind of mystical silence found in Neo-Platonism (in Plotinus, for example), in which the aim of the soul is to accommodate itself to an impersonal divine order and the kind of silence that involves a *listening to*.[20]

19. Chrétien, *The Ark of Speech*, 39.

20. Chrétien suggests that these are reflected in two quite distinct Greek words, *siōpē* and *sigē* respectively.

It is this quality of silent attentiveness that also distinguishes true speech from what we have heard Heidegger describe as "idle talk," since "To listen in silence, with all my silence, such indeed is the preface to every speech that is not mere chatter."[21] In fact, such genuine, attentive silence is itself eloquent, a kind of speaking. This is true not least in the case of prayer, which Chrétien describes as "a silence that is offered . . . to the one God who listens and sees, and not to a blind, anonymous Absolute[;] . . . a naked appearance before the Word . . . whose grace alone is what has made such dispositions possible in us."[22] Again, this is contrasted with the silence of Plotinus that, he suspects, "is surreptitiously nothing more than the adoration of the negation that suppresses our speech and thereby also our silence."[23] Christian silence, at least, is not simply a negation practiced upon our cognitive capacities: it is the silence of love.

Now we can begin to see why the deepening of Romanticism's lyric moment in the direction of the religious may appropriately be figured not simply as becoming attentive to silence but also as asking for a word. For a *word*, that is, a word that is attentive to the silence of the other and that speaks from and towards a silence that invites the word of the other, is a kind of communication well fitted to the exigencies of love. To find such a word is to learn not only how to speak but also how to listen, not only how to ask but also how to respond.[24]

To Kierkegaard's suspicious mind too much Romantic poetry never expressed more than empty longing and, as such, became a means of evading not only the social and intellectual challenges of an age of technology but also the self-knowledge and moral transformation required of those who would speak the heart's word in spirit and in truth. In Muir's terms, those who are satisfied with such poetry have not yet learned the heart-break that must precede heart-healing and heart-resurrection. Kierkegaard and Muir alike suggest that the lyric moment of Romanticism must be modulated by suffering and responsibility and make the difficult passage from song to word. Only so will we be able to speak forth the heart's need and only so will we be learning not only to speak our own word but also to be attentive to the word of the other. Whether a particular word, whether

21. Ibid., 57.

22. Ibid., 61.

23. Ibid., 69.

24. The theme of call and response is the subject of Chrétien's book *The Response and the Call*.

of a poet or a philosopher, of a Hölderlin or a Heidegger, is such a word is, of course, a judgment that can only be made in the light of how we attend to their words—but for as long as we are still listening, we must and will suspend our judgments. Whether Heidegger's coming God (or is it "god") is a God who might save us or even a God who might listen seems still an open question. But that very openness at least allows us to go on listening and invites us to listen all the more keenly and urgently, and that, at least, is something gained.

Looking in from the outside, who can say ever say whether a word that purports to be spoken from the heart is merely the expression of an empty longing or a confession of joy in the promise of a love without re-serve, whether it is the word of a poet giving voice to a spontaneous inner urge to speak or whether it is a word of prayer prayed "to" another? Isn't even the emptiest longing, in its way, a longing to live and to be fully pres-ent in what Vladimir Jankélévitch, that most lyrical of all modern European thinkers, called our "one chance in all eternity," "our one, unique spring morning"?[25] And, if so, isn't that at least bordering on prayer (even if it is not addressed *to* any "one")? It might be said that more is required of prayer than the need of the isolated individual, that we should pray not only for our individual "unique spring morning," but for the kingdom—as Jankélévitch too seems to acknowledge when he further specifies what we might long for as "an ecumenical good-will succeeding the Babel of univer-sal misunderstanding."[26] But isn't that already implicit within the longing for "our one, unique spring morning," making it an Easter morning? Who can say? who knows?—except the heart itself? Whether the lyric moment already is the incognito of prayer or prayer is to be reached by a certain deepening within the lyric moment, whether the lyric moment exists other than as the longing for the lyric moment or prayer exists other than as the longing to pray, are not questions that can easily be answered outside the dialogue of those who long for the one or the other, who seek the one in the other or the other in the one. If our hearts must break in order to learn a wider compassion, isn't the broken heart that once begins to speak already, in some sense, praying? But, then again, if we once began to pray and, in praying, let our hearts find their voice, would we still need "a god" to save us? Wouldn't we already have received what we were praying for? What else is there to pray to, what else is there to pray *for*, but the word that breaks,

25. Jankélévitch, *Le Je-ne-sais-quoi 1*, 147.
26. Jankélévitch, *Le Je-ne-sais-quoi 2*, 248.

heals, and resurrects the heart and teaches it to speak its word? In other words, what is there to pray for but prayer itself? What more might we ask for? But is even this still a possibility?

If prayer can only be prayed as a word from the heart, we have been put on notice how difficult it is to find true heart-words, since to speak them we would have to find our own inner point of unity (our heart!), and to remain true to it in our relations to others. And if we did find the courage to face our moral demons and challenge our relational and social woes, where in the complex artefactual technological mediation of language in our time might we find the words we need? Where, but in the heart? And how might such a word be spoken if not as "a new thing," a unique, creative occurrence, a new possibility coming into being independently of any preceding actuality? If these questions have real force, then this word must be a word that even when spoken will be said in secret since there is no existing frame of reference by which to define or interpret it; it will be a word that even when spoken remains, somehow, unsayable and as if unsaid. It may even be a word that sounds like silence. No doubt, such words need time—time to be spoken, time to be understood, time to be lived. "Time, merciful lord, / Grant us to hear your word"—and to speak our heart's word, one to another, each asking from each what each most wants to give and each striving to awaken in each what else would never be.

Muir, writing from within the era of existentialism—what Auden called "the age of anxiety"—undoubtedly experienced all that the existentialists did in relation to anxiety and thrownness towards death. Like them he also wrestled with the question of what poetry might mean in an age of desolation, of world wars, genocide, and a threatened nuclear holocaust. Yet, as we have seen, his exploration of time led him to the possibility that, in the end, time is not only time or not only time that is fated, as Berdyaev put it, to collapse in ruins. Time also gives the possibility for the heart to speak a word of prayer and, in this word of prayer, to speak also a word of love. For that we may be grateful.

Bibliography

Andersen, Hans Christian. *Eventyr. II: Nye Eventyr 1844–48*. Edited by E. Dal. Copenhagen: Reitzel, 1964.

Arendt, Hannah. *The Human Condition*. Chicago: University of Chicago Press, 1958.

Baron, Naomi, *Always On: Language in an Online and Mobile World*. Oxford: Oxford University Press, 2008.

Barr, James, *Biblical Words for Time*. London: SCM, 1962.

Benjamin, Walter. *Charles Baudelaire: A Lyric Poet in the Era of High Capitalism*. Translated by H. Zohn. London: New Left, 1973.

Berdyaev, Nicholas. *The Beginning and the End*. Translated by R. M. French. London: Bles, 1952.

———. *Slavery and Freedom*. Translated by R. M. French, London: Bles, 1943.

———. *Solitude and Society*. Translated by G. Reavey. London: Geoffrey Bles, 1938.

Broch, Hermann. *The Sleepwalkers*. Translated by Willa and Edwin Muir. London: Quartet, 1986.

Buber, Martin. *I and Thou*. Translated by W. Kaufmann. Edinburgh: T. & T. Clark, 1970.

Bultmann, Rudolf. *Das Evangelium des Johannes*. Göttingen: Vandenhoeck and Ruprecht, 1950.

———. *Theologische Enzyklopädie*. Tübingen: Mohr, 1984.

Caputo, John D. *Demythologizing Heidegger*. Bloomington: Indiana University Press, 1993.

Chrétien, Jean-Louis. *The Ark of Speech*. Translated by A. Brown. London: Routledge, 2004.

———. *The Call and the Response*. Translated by A. A. Davenport. New York: Fordham University Press, 2004.

Cupitt, Don. *Life, Life*. Santa Rosa CA: Polebridge, 2003.

Dreyfus, Hubert. *On the Internet*. London: Routledge, 2001.

Hegel, G. W. F. *Enzyklopädie der Philosophischen Wissenschaften*, Vol. II. G. W. F. Hegels Werke, vol. 9. Frankfurt am Main: Suhrkamp, 1986.

Heidegger, Martin. *Erläuterungen zu Hölderlins Dichtungen*. 1977. Reprint. Frankfurt: Klostermann, 1996.

———. *Being and Time*. Translated by J. Macquarrie and E. Robinson. Oxford: Blackwell, 1962.

———. *Unterwegs zur Sprache*. Stuttgart: Neske, 1959.

———. *What is Called Thinking?* New York: Harper and Row, 1968.

———. "Zeit und Sein." In *Zur Sache des Denkens*, 1–26. Tübingen. Niemeyer, 1969.

Henry, Michel. *L'Incarnation*. Paris: Éditions de Seuil, 2000.

Herbert, George. *The Works of George Herbert*. 2 vols. London: Pickering, 1846.

Hofmannsthal, Hugo von. *The Lord Chandos Letter and Other Writings*. Translated by J. Rotenberg. New York: New York Review of Books, 2005.

Hopkins, Gerard Manley. *Poems and Prose*. Edited by W. H. Gardner. Harmondsworth, UK: Penguin, 1953.

Jackson, Maggie, *Distracted*. Amherst, NY: Prometheus, 2008.

Jankélévitch, Vladimir. *Le Je-ne-sais-quoi et le Presque-rien 1: La manière et l'occasion*. Paris: Éditions du Seuil, 1980.

———. *Le Je-ne-sais-quoi et le Presque-rien 2: La méconaissance*. Paris: Éditions du Seuil, 1980.

Jarvis, Simon, *Wordsworth's Philosophic Song*. Cambridge: Cambridge University Press, 2007.

Keller, Helen. *The Story of My Life*. London: Hodder and Stoughton, 1959.

Kierkegaard, Søren. *The Concept of Anxiety*. Translated by R. Thomte. Princeton: Princeton University Press, 1980.

———. *Fear and Trembling*. Translated by H. V. and E. H. Hong. Princeton: Princeton University Press, 1983.

———. *Kierkegaard's Journals and Notebook*. Translated and edited by N. J. Cappelørn et al. Princeton: Princeton University Press, 2008.

———. *Kierkegaard's Spiritual Writings*. Translated by G. Pattison. New York: Harper and Row, 2010.

———. *The Point of View*. Edited and translated by H. V. and E. H. Hong. Princeton: Princeton University Press, 2009.

———. *Works of Love*. Translated by H. V. and E. H. Hong. New York: Harper, 2009.

Krishek, Sharon. *Kierkegaard on Faith and Love*. Cambridge: Cambridge University Press, 2009.

Marcel, Gabriel. *Tragic Wisdom and Beyond*. Translated by S. Jolin and P. McCormick. Evanston, IL: Northwestern University Press, 1973.

Moore, E. (nom de plume of Edwin Muir). *We Moderns: Enigmas and Guesses*. London: Heinemann, 1918.

Muir, Edwin. *Collected Poems*. London: Faber and Faber, 1960.

———. *Essays on Literature and Society*. London: Hogarth, 1965.

———. *John Knox: Portrait of a Calvinist*. London: Cape, 1930.

Muir, Willa. *Belonging: A Memoir*. London: Hogarth, 1968.

Nietzsche, Friedrich. *The Joyful Wisdom*. Translated by O. Levy. London: Foulis, 1910.

———. *The Will to Power*. Translated by W. Kaufmann. New York: Vintage, 1968.

Post, Laurens van der. *Venture to the Interior*. Harmondsworth, UK: Penguin, 1957.

Siegel, Lee. *Against the Machine: Being Human in the Age of the Electronic Mob*. London: Serpent's Tail, 2008.

Tillich, Paul. *The Boundaries of Our Being*. London: Fontana, 1973.

———. *Systematic Theology*. 3 vols. Welwyn, UK: Nisbet, 1968.

Turkle, Sherry. *Alone Together: Why We Expect More from Technology and Less from Each Other*. New York: Basic, 2011.

Wordsworth, William. *Poems*. Edited by P. Wayne. London: Dent, 1955.

Zum Brunn, Emilie. *St. Augustine: Being and Nothingness*. New York: Paragon House, 1986.

Index of Names and Subjects

Index of Scripture